BARRY R. STROHM

SPIRITS
SPEAK
OF THE UNIVERSE

EXTRATERRESTRIALS, SPIRITUALITY, AND OUR GALAXY

4880 Lower Valley Road • Atglen, PA 19310

I believe alien life is quite common in the universe, although intelligent life is less so. Some say it has yet to appear on planet Earth.

—STEVEN HAWKING

The more I learn of the miracle of the journey of the soul through the eons of time, the more I am aware of how the lives of soul mates intertwine during their incarnate experiences. To Connie, my wife of fifty-two years, my soul mate and emotional anchor in this lifetime. Without her help and encouragement, whatever little I have been able to accomplish would not have been possible. The guides have told us that we have been together in seven prior lifetimes. My heart tells me that we will be together many more times in the future, on both sides of the veil.

I also want to dedicate this book to my alien spirit mentor and friend, Mou. He has provided the information for my prior book, *Aliens Among Us: Exploring Past and Present* as well as the great detail of all things extraterrestrial in this book. The information he has provided has only been limited by my ability to understand what he was saying. Hopefully, I will someday be better able to comprehend his teachings, maybe in a future lifetime.

Published by Schiffer Publishing, Ltd.
4880 Lower Valley Road
Atglen, PA 19310
Phone: (610) 593-1777; Fax: (610) 593-2002
E-mail: Info@schifferbooks.com
Web: www.schifferbooks.com

For our complete selection of fine books on this and related subjects, please visit our website at www.schifferbooks.com. You may also write for a free catalog.

Schiffer Publishing's titles are available at special discounts for bulk purchases for sales promotions or premiums. Special editions, including personalized covers, corporate imprints, and excerpts, can be created in large quantities for special needs. For more information, contact the publisher.

We are always looking for people to write books on new and related subjects. If you have an idea for a book, please contact us at proposals@schifferbooks.com.

CONTENTS

ACKNOWLEDGMENTS

Our primary means of spirit communication is a special channeling board. Our board is based on a design attributed to Sam and Carol Green of Salt Lake City, Utah. Their use of the board dates back more than forty years. We were taught the use of the channeling board by their daughters, K. Kivett and Sammi Tall. During the process of gathering information for this book we would channel over Skype with K and her husband Doc, or during live sessions with Sammi. Their patience and instruction has allowed Connie and me to advance the practice of this type of spirit communication. We also value the continued participation of the spirit of Carol Green since she has passed over.

A new contributor to our circle of psychics is Donna Daacke. Donna has been participating in our channeling sessions and has brought her mental energies to supplement the information gained from the board. She has unique talents and her contributions are greatly appreciated. We look forward to working with her in the future.

None of the information published in this book would be possible without the contributions of knowledge from the spirit guides. For those of you unfamiliar with spirit guides, they are souls on the other side of the life veil that possess unique abilities to provide information concerning past, present, and future events. There is a chapter in this book on reincarnation that will help you to better understand the path of the human soul and the information that becomes available to those souls willing to help others.

Perhaps the most unique spirit to assist in this book is named Mou. In his prior life, he was an alien that actually visited our planet on several occasions. He provided much of the information in my prior book, *Aliens Among Us: Exploring Past and Present*, and this book as well. I have an entire chapter dedicated to Mou and I think you will enjoy his humor and knowledge. Many other guides also contributed information, and I would like to note a special thanks to Raz, Sterling, Rachel, Tim, and other spiritual participants.

PREFACE

In this book you will learn the real truth in great detail about the alien presence here on Earth, what they contributed in the past, are currently contributing, and what their plans are for the future of humans. Topics of conversation include the universality of God and spirituality; reincarnation; and life in our solar system, galaxy, and the universe. Also, discussed in detail are travel in space, extraterrestrial vehicles, and alien types.

Our special channeling board. Barry Strohm.

We use our gift of spirit communication to bring you information provided by the soul of an extraterrestrial as well as other master guides. Our tool for detailed communication with the spirits is a channeling board, which dates to ancient China and has persisted through human evolution to the present. Native Americans even use a basic form of it. Everyone is probably familiar with the Ouija Board, complete with stories of associated evil presences. Our board is unique, the configuration of the board was derived from a channeling session where we allowed the spirit guides to design the physical features of the board. It's configuration of letters, numbers, and words is shown above. It is round and has a glass surface to facilitate the movement of a small glass cup, similar to a shot glass. We initiate all sessions with a prayer of protection that was also given to us by the spirits. We always maintain a video and audio of all spirit communication and prepare a written transcript. As this book goes to press, we have channeled more than 400 hours and have communicated with spirits ranging from saints to aliens.

We were introduced to our alien spirit friend by the name of Mou in the summer of 2014, during a channeling session with our friends in Salt Lake City, K and Doc Kivett. They had introduced us to the concept of board channeling with spirits and spirit guides several years earlier. Their family has been using this technique of spirit communication for more than forty years. Under their guidance, Connie (my wife) and I have advanced remarkably in our journey of soul experiences and learning. Without them, very little of this book would have been possible.

In this book, we provide information about alien species that range from Arcturians to Zetas. Alien types are discussed in precise detail that will give the reader an understanding into who is really observing us and what their mission is here on Earth. There is a chapter dedicated to the various alien vehicles and a discussion on why they are invisible to human eyes, as well as how these vehicles traverse huge distances between galaxies. The reality of alien shape-shifters and their physical presence among us is another point of discussion. We will even discuss the future and the human role in space exploration.

Our Solar System

Our solar system. Adobe Stock.

In one chapter, I examine the planets of our solar system and attempt to show how relative distances, as we comprehend them, compare to our galaxy and the Universe. Many of the facts concerning the planets in our solar system are quite intriguing. For instance, did you know that the density of Saturn is so light that it would actually float in water or that Jupiter is so big you could fit 1,300 Earths inside of it? I inquire of Mou, the alien spirit, what is actually taking place on these planets and whether they support intelligent life now or in past times.

As our scientific knowledge increases and the use of our technology allows us to see deeper into the Universe, there are many new mysteries to be solved. For instance, did you know that Jupiter has a moon covered in ice, and there is an ocean under the ice that could actually have a moderate temperature? Our astronomers have discovered a star whose light has dimmed by more than twenty percent during the last several years, as if a large, extraterrestrial structure has blocked the light from the star. We ask our alien spirit to answer many of the mysteries of the Universe.

Imagine the Unimaginable

The immensity of the Universe is unimaginable. The picture below is that of our galaxy, the Milky Way. There are billions of galaxies in our universe. On a much smaller scale, our space probe, Voyager 1 was launched in 1977. It took thirty-five years to reach the beginning of interstellar space, the place where the sun's magnetic field stops affecting its surrounding matter. Scientists believe interstellar space begins 12,250,000,000 miles from the sun. Voyager 1 will have to travel another 40,000 years until it encounters our nearest star. Comparisons such as this give some idea of scale of our planet when compared to the stars around us. Not only is the size of our universe unimaginable, our scientists say it is expanding.

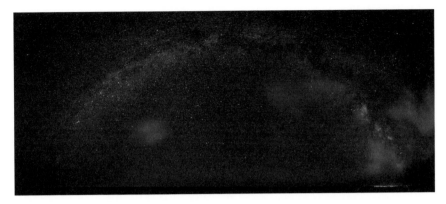

Our Galaxy, the Milky Way. Adobe Stock.

Aliens Also Have Souls

If you have read my prior book, *Aliens Among Us: Exploring Past and Present*, you will already know that aliens have the same souls as humans and go to the same Heaven upon their passing from incarnate lives. Since they have souls, we can use our gift of spirit communication to open channels with our guides and obtain information from them. If you have *not* read my earlier books, you are probably having a choking fit over the last statement. In any event, you are about to embark on an informational journey that will require an open mind and some imagination—in certain instances, a lot of imagination. When you open your mind, anything is possible.

I know from statements made in reviews of my previous books that skeptics will only seek to find arguments about why the information contained in this book cannot possibly be true. Not too many years ago, I would count myself in that group of individuals. The concept of being able to converse on a regular basis with an alien spirit takes a lot of getting used to. Since alien disclosure by our governments is far from a current reality, I must concede that there is really no way of scientifically proving the statements and comments in this book. There is also no way to *disprove* this information. Only time can verify if what we are told will come to fruition. Keep in mind that we have been told that my writing and publishing these books is part of the disclosure process.

The comment I hear most is, "How do you know you are really talking to an alien?" When we were first introduced to Mou, the alien spirit, I also had serious doubts about the authenticity of the information we were receiving. It is very difficult to test a spirit about alien information when you have no personal knowledge of the subject. In the beginning, all sessions were conducted by Skype where the board was located with K and Doc in Salt Lake City, UT, and I was in Pennsylvania asking the questions. My friends on the channeling board had no knowledge of the subject matter of the questions, and having the board more than 2,100 miles away certainly negated any influence I would have on the answers. I was astonished by the knowledge Mou had of what I was doing back in Pennsylvania.

By the third time we channeled with Mou, he had appeared to me as a blue flash and verified what I had seen immediately during the next session. I tell that story in the next chapter, *My Friend, Mou*. I would ask very detailed questions of him, and his answers appeared very logical and sometimes understandable. We have now channeled with my spirit friend more than one hundred hours, and the information he has given is the basis for two books about the extraterrestrial presence. Every word that you are about to read is recorded on video and audio in my files as proof of the source of the information contained herein and not a product of my imagination.

Our Alien Spirit Appears

Our journey of learning about the other intelligent beings in our universe began during a channeling session with K and Doc in July of 2014. I had started to write my first alien book but was struggling with obtaining the proper information from our regular spirit guides. As part of the session, I was complaining to the guide that there was no way I could write about something of which I had such little knowledge. He replied:

> *No one does so we are going to teach you. We are going to dictate most of it, or we should say a new teacher. Yes, his name is Mou.*

I thought that was a strange name for a guide but let it slide for the moment. At that time I was considering combining a book about aliens with a book about historical conspiracies. When I inquired if the alien book should be kept separate, the guide added a little more detail to his earlier statement.

> *Mou is good at that subject; he is one.*

Not exactly the answer I was expecting! In order to clarify if I had heard correctly, I asked if my new guide was really an alien. His answer was short and to the point.

> *Yes.*

After a little hesitation and consideration about how to reply to that information I said, "I would love to meet him."

> *He is dead! Ha, ha, ha. Mou will need to learn this [meaning the spirit board]. He will begin to talk to you.*

It took Connie and me a little time to digest the fact that we were actually going to have the chance to communicate with the spirit of a real alien. We were able to talk to him, and he would additionally exhibit an astonishing ability to assist in my writing. I would also point out that by this time our daughters were convinced we were both totally crazy, and each book I write seems to reinforce that opinion.

Not only did he supply us with amazing information on the channeling board, but he gave us personal messages showing he had a great knowledge of what was happening in the world around Connie and me.

In many instances, he has predicted events that would take place for both Connie and myself. He definitely looks out for our best interests. Many of the future predictions that I send out to my email subscription list have come from our alien guide. My email subscribers have been getting information from an alien spirit for quite a while. I insinuated they were from a normal guide rather than having all my subscribers think I was totally out of my mind.

Much of what you are about to read has never appeared in print before. Many of the questions asked require understanding far beyond our knowledge. For instance, one night I asked a question and was told he could not describe an emotion that was never felt by humans. He also said he was "dumbing down" the information given me for my own safety. Mou is quite aware of the extremes taken by our governments to protect the alien secret. Cultures on other planets have a head start on humans measured in millenniums. Their technology is incredible as compared to our own. If the visitors from other planets wished to harm us, we would be harmed.

A problem with humans is their inability to imagine life that does not conform to the model of life we see around us. We have to keep in mind that life in other environments may not look like or have the same requirements as on our planet. For instance, in life, Mou breathed a nitrogen-rich atmosphere. There may be cultures that have no requirement for oxygen in their atmosphere. Our scientists search for planets that have characteristics similar to Earth. It is possible another life form may breathe methane or a gas with which we are totally unfamiliar. The atmosphere of Venus is carbon-dioxide and sulfuric-acid. Consider the possibility that there may be beings that consider that mix the perfect atmosphere. Where humans require a moderate temperature range, others might be very comfortable at -200 degrees—as you will see in this book, if you can imagine it, it is possible.

In other chapters, I investigate the concept of a universal deity and what cultures on other planets think of spirituality. In another, we look into the possibility that soul energy is capable of reincarnating throughout the galaxy. We explore the concept of travel in deep space and how it is accomplished, in spite of the incredible distances that have to be transversed. As mentioned, space vehicles are examined in detail, from one the size of the United States to drones the size of baseballs. In one chapter, I include personal photographs of an actual alien drone that followed me one evening in Gettysburg, Pennsylvania. The alien types that travel in these vehicles are discussed in depth.

This book will give the reader a unique opportunity to learn and hopefully understand much about what is taking place around us in the incredible Universe. You can open your mind and imagine the miracles, or you can remain close-minded and fail to understand the journey of the soul and humanity as it attempts to become more like our all-powerful God and the evolution of mankind in their attempt to travel the stars.

CHAPTER 1

MY FRIEND, MOU

Mou is a spirit that, in his last life, was a "blue alien." For the last couple of years, he has helped me write one book that has been published previously, *Aliens Among Us: Exploring Past and Present*, and he is the primary information source in this current volume. Even though his last life was on a planet many light years away, he has the same soul as humans on Earth. I know I am repeating myself, but our gift of spirit communication has allowed us to communicate with him utilizing our channeling board.

As you will see in more detail in other chapters, he reincarnates in the same manner as humans and worships the same God that we worship here on Earth. In many ways he reflects a universal norm in attempting to get galactic beings to just "get along." Thousands of years ago he even came back as a human and lived a lifetime here on this planet. He has a great sense of humor and exhibits it in our interviews. His depth of knowledge will astound and is only limited by our inability to understand the sometimes complex information he is providing.

Mou Is Blue

We started by asking Mou to describe himself when he was in body. He replied:

> *Tall, thin, with large eyes and a bluish skin. Small ears and small nose, big mouth. Hands have four fingers and a thumb like yours. Our feet are the same, our feet are hands. You cannot tell sexes by looking.*

"When you had a body, how tall did you stand?"

> *In your measurements, just over 9 feet tall.*

No doubt that when he was in body, he would stand out in a crowd. I inquired how long the people lived on his planet.

> *We live in your time about 1,000 years. We are not adults until we are 300.*

Talk about living to a ripe old age! They live almost twelve times longer than humans. Mou is a spirit presence and is on the other side of the life veil. I asked in what year he passed.

> *1987. OK. And your time I was 942. My planet 159. Our rotation around our two suns is much longer. We have twin stars as our suns.*

When I asked him about his family life and how many wives he had, the response was:

Three. HaHaHa. On my planet we males are born less often. About 5 to 1. This way less food and things are used.

He apparently thought it was funny to have three wives. As I write this chapter, Connie and I have celebrated fifty-two years of marriage, and I cannot imagine having more than one wife, or even living for more than 950 years. Next, I inquired the name of his home planet. He replied:

We call it Robbe.

He went on to tell us the total population on his planet is only about nine billion beings. There are limited resources there and everything is in an ecological balance. When I asked him where his planet was located his answer was:

Out on the farthest arm of the Milky Way. On the tip there is a planet the size of your Jupiter. It has 8 moons and twin suns.

That is a really big planet. Jupiter's mass is huge, more than 300 times that of Earth. One evening we decided to ask him some more personal questions. Having never had a good look at him other that seeing the blue flash, I asked him if he wore clothes.

No.

That opened a whole world of possibilities, but I decided not to pursue that line of questioning any longer. I inquired if he used his mouth to eat.

No.

"Do you use your mouth to speak words?"

No.

"How do you communicate?"

I cannot explain since humans have never experienced.

Once again, he alluded to how limited our human experiences are. I guess this is why he is spending so much time trying to educate us. In a later session I tried to bring up the subject of how they communicated. This time I think he tried to oversimplify for my convenience. He replied:

Thoughts.

"Like mental telepathy?"

As you would refer.

My guess is that he figured out that such an answer would appease me on the subject. Next, I asked if his ears were for hearing sounds. He replied:

Yes.

At least we have one feature in common.

Life on Robbe

Life on Robbe is certainly going to be very different from life on our planet. I thought I would investigate more about life in his world. "Can you tell me more about life on your planet?"

We breathe a nitrogen rich gas. We live mostly subsurface but our food grows on land. Water is not like yours. Every morning it rains.

"Can you explain how your water differs from ours?"

H_3O, heavier. Does not freeze in low temperatures. It has to drop pretty cold to freeze.

When I inquired as to the total population of his planet, he answered:

In your number, 9 billion.

The population of Earth is around 7.5 billion people. When you compare size, the diameter of Jupiter is more than eleven times that of Earth; its volume is 1,300 times that of our planet, so you can see that Mou comes from a very large planet, but when compared with the size and population of Earth, it is sparsely populated.

Earth compared to the size of Jupiter. Adobe Stock.

On our planet, there are many different types of humans. When I asked if there were different types on his planet, the answer was:

Same.

"Do your people have jobs?

Duties.

Is there any crime on your planet?"

No.

I have referred to the blues as a very advanced culture; having no crime would certainly be very advanced for earthlings. Next, I asked him if any individuals ever fight on his planet. He responded:

Have evolved past conflict. We are peaceful.

It is becoming easy to understand why the extraterrestrials like to visit our planet; it gives them the opportunity to view "fight night" every day. My next question was, "Do you live in a home like we do?"

No.

"Can you explain?

Not required. There is no need for shelter.

He did mention that they mostly lived underground. I know that one of my great personal weaknesses is liking to consume food, a lot of it quite fattening. My next question addressed if the "blues" need to eat.

Not like eat.

"Do they have food?'

No.

Obviously no fine restaurants on his planet! My mind was having a problem grasping not having food. My follow up question was, "Do they need nourishment?'

Yes.

"How do they get the required nourishment?"

Minerals absorbed.

Being a bit overweight myself, I thought I would find out if anyone was overweight on his planet. He replied:

No.

Connie and I just rescued two kittens so I decided it would be a good time to ask Mou if they had any pets on his planet. His answer was:

Yes.

"Are they similar to our pets?"

Subspecies.

Since at the time, we were trying to keep up with two kittens, I inquired if they have any cats on Robbe.

Not as such.

"Can you describe them?

Describing nothing you have seen before.

That answer certainly opens the door to your imagination. I should have asked him how many feet their cats have. We had not discussed how people got around on his planet so I asked, "How do people travel on your planet?"

On our planet we walk or ride energy streams. To fly, almost all crafts look alike. It is because it is the most effective method. I do not reinvent the world. OK!

The concept of riding an energy stream is quite intriguing. It certainly makes more sense than driving a car on a highway.

Call Me

The first time I was introduced to him, he gave me the following message:

I am here because you called me. When you write, about an hour before, you need to call upon me. This way I can get into your head and see what you write. If I do not like what you say or the way you say it, I can give you a sign, like an itchy nose or blurry eyes. I am certain we will be as one.

I soon realized he actually could get into my mind and assist in my writing. And yes, he can really make my nose itch on occasions. A couple of nights later we were channeling, and I asked him if he was helping me transcribe my notes and work on the book. He answered:

I was, and enjoying your mind, too.

He is probably the only soul in the galaxy that is enjoying my mind. If I ever had any doubts that he knew what I was writing in my books, one night I asked him what he thought of them. His answer reflected just how involved he really was with my writing.

OK, now to the book. You need to add a bit to a few chapters. You are lacking explanation. You are going to leave the readers on a cliff if you do not add a few sentences to explain your conclusions. Skim through it and I will point out what I am saying.

When I went back through the draft of the book, certain areas did need extra work and his comments were correct. I made the changes and the next time we channeled, he was satisfied with the changes we made together. His abilities are truly astonishing.

Breakfast Appearance

When we had just been first introduced, I thought I would see if he really could help me write. I was finishing the final chapter of *Aliens Among Us: Exploring Past and Present* and was having trouble getting it right. I mentally asked Mou if he could help me write the chapter and sat down in front of the computer. The words seemed to flow and the chapter was finished in about three hours. Connie does my proofing and read the chapter. She commented about how my writing was improving. I just nodded and agreed with her.

The next morning, we decided to go to a local family restaurant for breakfast. As we were sitting there waiting for our meals, I commented that I was sure I had help the night before while writing the chapter. Suddenly, there was a bright flash of blue light in the chair next to me at the table. Connie did not see it, but I told her I thought that Mou had just appeared to me in the form of a blurred light. She thought I was a little nuts. A couple of days later we were scheduled to channel using Skype with our friends in Salt Lake City. They would have the board and I was going to ask a question for the book. With the board 2,000 miles away there was no danger of me influencing the answers. I made a point of not mentioning the blue flash of light or the interactions I was having with Mou. The session began with me making a request for the presence of Mou. While I watched the Skype video connection, the following message was spelled out.

Hello from the blue flash.

My friends had absolutely no idea of what had taken place in Pennsylvania! He had confirmed that the blue flash of light was indeed my spirit friend making his presence known.

Looking Out for Connie

A couple of years ago, we were preparing to go to Florida to spend Christmas with our family. In the last session before leaving, he told me the following:

Time for family now. After tonight, no, no, no, no, no work. Play. It is time for family and a special thank you to your wife, who puts up with us. You will, will, will take her out to dinner. Just the two of you and no, no, no, work talk. Tell her how pretty she is. OK, OK.

On the evening we started the drive south, we stopped at one of our favorite places to eat in Maryland. As we finished ordering our meal, I realized that my nose started to itch in what was now becoming a familiar manner. I said to Connie, "You look really pretty tonight," to which she answered, "Thanks, Mou." As soon as I said it, my nose stopped itching! Our blue friend was apparently accompanying us on our nice dinner and was pleased I was following his directions.

In several instances, he has actually tried to act as our protector. During a session one night, he warned Connie that she was going to fall in the near future. When she asked if she was going to take a fall in the store, he answered in the negative. We tried to get additional information, but he would say no more, only that she needed to be careful. About a week later we had a snow storm move through the area. It was just enough snow to cover an ice spot in front of our apartment. Connie tried to take out our garbage and found out the hard way the location of the snow-covered ice spot. Her feet went out from under her and she landed squarely on her posterior with no damage to anything but her dignity. Several nights later, we were channeling with Mou, and Connie mentioned that now she realized what he was referring to with her falling. Mou replied:

Yes, and did you notice I made you fall on your butt so you did not hurt yourself.

I tried very hard not to laugh at his answer. Did I mention that Mou has a very good sense of humor? During another session, Mou proved his amazing capability to be aware of what was going on around us here at our store in New Oxford, Pennsylvania. He stated:

You need to boost your immune system, somebody sneezed on you.

Earlier in the day, a customer had come into the store and had sneezed loudly and uncontrolled close to Connie. Our blue friend was once again attempting to look out for her.

I Do Not Kiss and Tell

There was a period of a couple of weeks where we could not make contact with him on the channeling board. The other guides told us that he was not there. We started to get a little worried, but the next time I requested his presence, we received this message.

Hey, back. I am back.

I explained that we were worried about him, then I asked if he was on a hot date.

Two, but I do not kiss and tell.

Our blue alien is a true gentleman! I was going to ask him what "blues" do on a date, but I decided that in this case discretion was the better part of valor.

The more time we spent with Mou, the more we realized there was no way to anticipate his next message. One evening as I was gathering information for this book, I requested Mou's presence so I could ask him some questions. He came in by saying:

I have a full name.

When I asked him what it was, he replied:

Moutuior. Now, how's that. In your sounds. I realize Mou is easier.

Not wanting to hurt his feelings, I asked, "Is that how you want us to refer to you in the future?"

No.

Now I was puzzled why he would give us his name if he did not want us to use it. I asked him if he was upset that we have not been using his proper name.

Oh, no. It is just time for a formal introduction.

The next time we had a channeling session, I asked the guide that was working with us at the time if Mou was present?

Rounding him up.

When he came through, I addressed him as Moutuior and asked him if I was pronouncing it correctly. He replied:

Sure, but I like Mou.

"I thought if I got it right I would impress you. Are you hard to impress?"

Na.

Since that time we have only referred to him as Mou.

Not Very High-Tech

The more we got to know Mou, the more we came to expect the unexpected. With all his technical knowledge, we thought he was familiar with all our recent breakthroughs in technology, especially our smart phones. One evening we were Skype channeling with K and Doc in Salt Lake City. Connie and I again were in Pennsylvania. On that evening, we began the session by asking Mou if he would like to make a statement. Here was his answer:

Hi to all. I have a young soul that I have been talking with that is trying to teach me cell short cuts the kids use on their cell phones. He says if we learn it we can save time on this. But I can only remember a few, like LOL. I guess I am a lost cause. We are getting too old. I guess in my next life it is one of the things to do. OK. But I gave you LOL.

I guess the blues are far more advanced than texting on cell phones. Sometime I think it is very similar on both sides of the life veil. I wonder if there is a law about flying a space craft while texting?

Photographing a Blue

When I was writing my third book, *Aliens Among Us: Exploring Past and Present*, I decided that it would be nice to include a photograph of my blue spirit friend. When I asked him if he would pose for a picture for the book, he informed me that I already had two pictures of him in my files. Apparently he had posed for the photographs several years earlier while I was doing the photos for my first book, *Haunting and History of the Battle of Gettysburg*. As soon as he made that statement, Connie mentioned that she thought she knew which picture he was referring to. I had been using a photograph of a blue streak of light in my lectures, stating that the source of the light was a mystery. Now the mystery was being solved. I pulled up the photograph from my files and added it to the book. During the next session

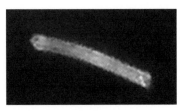

A second photograph of the spirit Mou. Barry Strohm.

I asked him if the picture Connie was referring to was the right one. He said:

Yes, it is a grand likeness of me.

Photograph of the spirit Mou, the blue flash. Barry Strohm.

When I asked if he would like a copy of the picture, he responded:

All the lady blue streaks would be jealous. Ha, ha, ha. Your photos would be streaked.

My guess he was quite a ladies' man in his last lifetime on Robbe. He did mention earlier that he had three wives.

I Got Your Back

Whenever I am doing a guest appearance on a radio show or writing about an extraterrestrial subject, I am aware that he is with me. On radio shows the words just seem to flow whenever the topic is aliens. In the summer of 2016, I was scheduled to speak at the Alien Cosmic Expo near Toronto, Canada. It was going to be the first time that I spoke in front of a live audience about extraterrestrials. I asked Mou if he would be going to Canada with us and he replied:

Indeed.

"Are we going to wow the Canadians?"

Yes.

He usually knows what I am writing or working on so I asked him if he approved of my presentation. His answer was once again:

Yes.

It is always nice to know that he approves of what I am doing. At the end of that session, I finished by telling him that I appreciated all he did for us and that I would need him in Canada. I felt a lot better when he said:

I got your back.

Not bad knowing you can count on a nine-foot alien spirit to cover your back. Since that time I have done numerous radio shows where I know his presence has assisted in answering questions. On several occasions he has joined us to do live board channeling during interviews, and we have even let callers ask questions. I can only hope that he will continue to assist us for many years to come.

Party Time

I thought I would pursue whether "blues" share any partying instincts with humans. I know that a drink during happy hour is quite relaxing for humans. I asked him if his alien type enjoys a drink.

Yes.

What do "blues" drink when they want to get drunk?

Cunsh.

Never heard of that before! I inquired what it was made of.

Emeleberries.

By this time I should have realized it was not going to be something that was familiar to humans. Next I asked, "Does it taste good?"

Nope, icky.

So even the advanced cultures put up with bad-tasting drinks to get a little buzz. He is always telling me that something is an emotion or feeling that we have never experienced. From this conversation I would come to the conclusion that getting inebriated is a galactic phenomenon.

Quotes by Mou

During our numerous channeling sessions, when I would be preparing for radio interviews, I would ask him if there were any statements that he would like me to read to help inform the public. Many of his statements turned out to be quite prophetic.

One night I asked him why it was important that humans evolve. He replied:

> *In the space time continuum there are as many virgin planets waiting to be settled or create their own karma as there is dead and worn out planets ready to be re eaten by its suns. The planets are on a timer. They are born, they thrive, and then they die. It is the way of things. In a few more billion years this solar system will be all burned up. Not from mans' misuse but just because that is the way of things. If we are to survive we need to learn to travel the stars. This is how and why you must learn not to depend on Earth forever. We are here to make sure you grow towards this.*

Many people fear the presence of aliens and believe, upon their arrival, the extraterrestrials will conquer humans and take over our planet. One evening he stressed the beneficial mission of the beings from space.

> *We are here to help you. We do not want your planet. We have our own thank you, and we do not want to harm you. This is all nonsense that we want what you have. We are here to make sure you can make the leap when you are ready.*

One other topic that I found particularly interesting was why they did not become involved with bringing peace among the different factions of humans. Instead, they seemed to almost encourage the violence that takes place on our planet. When I addressed this fact, he basically said that we need to learn our lessons the hard way.

> *There is always going to be conflict and in conflict we learn compromise. This is now what your world is now evolving into. Through war we learn peace.*

It looks like conflict is going to be a characteristic of earthlings for a very long time. As you can see from this chapter, Connie and I have grown to have a very deep affection for our blue alien friend. He has provided protection and insight into many of our problems. His information has been accurate, timely, and has now generated two books. We have even found out that our souls have been together in prior lifetimes. Through the miracle of reincarnation, we have shared lifetimes together in the past and hopefully will be sharing more in the future. He told us that our time with him would be limited to around two years and as I write this chapter we are approaching that time. I fear we will soon be saying goodbye to our blue friend. Hopefully, he will be there when we cross over. I am looking forward to seeing what he really looks like.

CHAPTER 2

OUR SOLAR SYSTEM

Before writing this chapter, I had no idea how to compare the relative size of our solar system and its planets to the vastness of deep space. In this chapter, I am going to take a look at our own solar system, compare the relative sizes of the planets, and let you know what my alien spirit has to say about each of them. Our solar system is located in the Milky Way galaxy, approximately 26,000 light years from its center. It consists of one sun, eight major planets, five recognized dwarf planets, approximately 3,400 comets, 470 natural satellites or moons, and more than 700,000 minor planets—and maybe even a planet or two that have not as yet been discovered. There is a lot of other crap out there too numerous to mention. It stands to reason that there must be a lot of stuff that is undiscovered. New asteroids or meteors are discovered every day, some coming relatively close to Earth.

One evening I asked if there were any undiscovered planets in our solar system. The guide replied:

3.

The closest star to our Earth is Proxima Centauri, a mere 4.22 light years away. To get an idea just how small our solar system is in relation to the Universe, Pluto is 3.7 billion miles from the sun. This distance equates to 0.00063 light year. Our Milky Way galaxy is more than 100,000 light years in width and has around 300 billion stars. A recent analysis by a German computer states that there could be as many as 500 billion galaxies in the Universe. Mou summed it up pretty well one night when he said:

Think of the possibilities.

When I started this chapter, I did not realize how little I knew about our solar system. I am going to discuss each of the planets in the order of their distance from the sun and give you a short synopsis of what the scientists tell us about them and, in some instances, their moons. Then, I will ask questions of Mou as well as other guides to see what is really taking place in our solar system.

Mercury

Mercury is the planet closest to the sun with an orbit around the sun every eighty-eight days. It has almost no atmosphere and a range in temperature from -280

Mercury, the planet nearest the sun. Adobe Stock.

degrees Fahrenheit at night to 800 degrees Fahrenheit during the day. Keep in mind that water boils at 212 degrees. For those of you who like temperature change, that is a swing of 1,100 degrees in a single day, unmatched in our solar system. It is relatively small in size with a radius of 1,516 miles, just slightly larger than our moon.

The surface of Mercury appears a lot like that of our moon with many craters. An asteroid around sixty miles in diameter struck the planet around 4 billion years ago, leaving a huge crater about the size of Texas. On Earth, we have a relatively thick atmosphere that protects us from much of the smaller meteors. Since Mercury has relatively no atmosphere, there is nothing to protect it from impacts.

Despite the high temperatures, in 2012, our NASA *Messenger* spacecraft discovered ice in the craters located near the northern pole. These craters are apparently shielded from the intense heat of the sun. That would seem to indicate that there might be an area on the planet of moderate temperature as well as the presence of water. I asked the guide if there was life on Mercury. He answered my question with a question.

Are you talking about intelligent life?

I re-phrased the question and asked if there was intelligent life on Mercury.

Not at this time.

Has there ever been life there?

No.

Do aliens currently use the planet for any of their operations?

No.

Mercury is so inhospitable, even the extraterrestrials appear to not want any part of it.

Venus

Venus, our morning and evening "star."
Adobe Stock.

One of the least hospitable planets in the solar system is Venus. Since it has an elliptical orbit, the distance to Earth varies from 162 million miles at its most distant orbit to as close as 24 million miles. It has an incredibly thick atmosphere consisting of carbon dioxide and sulfuric acid. Venus has the heaviest atmosphere of any planet in our solar system with a surface pressure almost ninety times the atmospheric pressure on Earth. Readily visible from Earth as what we call the morning and evening star, it is the planet second closest to the sun and has a radius of 3,760 miles, very similar in size to Earth. The high visibility is caused by the rays of the sun being reflected off the heavy atmosphere and its relatively close proximity to our planet.

As if the nature of the atmosphere is not enough of a deterrent to life, temperatures on the planet can reach 870 degrees Fahrenheit. Lead will melt at that temperature. Once on the surface, there are literally thousands of volcanoes, many of which are quite large and active. To a human, this would appear as one of the most uninhabitable places in the solar system. I started off by asking Mou if there is currently life of Venus. His answer was:

No.

However, when I asked him if there ever was life on Venus, he replied:

Yes.

It is generally believed that our solar system is 4.6 billion years old and our galaxy more than 13 billion years old, so a lot of changes have taken place during that time. When I asked why life ended on Venus, the reply was:

Sun.

"Are you saying the heavy atmosphere blocked the light from the sun?"

Yes.

Apparently even the most inhospitable planets have had periods where it could have supported life, but changes in the atmosphere created the conditions seen today.

Earth, Home Sweet Home

Earth, the best hope for intelligent life.
Adobe Stock.

Earth is the third planet from the sun and the densest planet in the solar system. It has a single moon that influences the ocean tides. It is the ebb and flow of the oceans that supports life. It orbits around the sun every 365.26 days and has a radius of 3,959 miles. The axis is tilted 23.4 degrees from perpendicular. It is this tilt that creates the seasons on Earth as different parts receive direct rays of the sun. A fact that I found very interesting is that the core temperature of our planet is 10,800 degrees Fahrenheit, similar to the temperature of the surface of the sun. This hot core is probably leftover since the time of the creation of the Earth, and the mantle has cooled over time. Scientists tell us the Earth has cooled approximately one degree C every 10 million years. I have no clue what the margin for error is in that computation. Maybe it will offset global warming.

The planet was believed to be formed 4.54 billion years ago and has undergone many physical changes. One interesting fact is that more than ninety-nine percent of the life species that have ever lived on Earth are extinct, an indication of just how much conditions have changed on this planet over the millenniums. Temperatures on Earth currently vary from a minimum of -128 degrees to a maximum of 135 degrees with a mean temperature of around 60 degrees. The planet is populated by approximately 7.4 billion humans but there is much discussion concerning if these earthlings really represent intelligent life.

At the present time, seventy-one percent of the area of the planet is water and twenty-nine percent is land mass. It is believed that water totally covered the Earth until about 2.5 billion years ago. One of the great mysteries concerning our world is how so much water came to cover our planet. I thought I would check this out with Mou. When I asked him if water was present at the time of creation of Earth, he answered:

It was but in a different form.

"What do you mean by it was a different form?"

Gas.

"If gas was present at the creation of Earth, how was it transformed to water?"

Falling temperatures.

"So you are saying that as Earth cooled, the falling temperatures converted the gas to water?"

Yes.

I was very happy that I finally received an answer that was relatively easy to understand.

Our Moon, It Rang Like a Bell

Earth's moon. Adobe Stock.

The density of the moon is 3.34 grams per cubic centimeter, which is much lighter than Earth at 5.51 grams per cubic centimeter. Scientists believe that the moon has a crust around thirty-one miles (fifty kilometers) in depth and a small solid core.

In the early days of our space exploration, we crashed objects into the moon and recorded the seismic effect. According to one report, the moon "rang like a bell" during one of the impacts. When I attempted to research what had truly happened, I ran into this article on the *Popular Science* website.

But something interesting happened on Apollo 12. After Pete Conrad and Al Bean landed at the Ocean of Storms on November 14, 1969, they left the lunar surface 142 hours into the flight. Eight hours later, they were reunited with Dick Gordon in the command module and sent their spent lunar module back to the Moon. It impacted about 40 miles away from the Apollo 12 landing site with the force of one ton of TNT. The resulting shockwave built up and peaked in just eight minutes. Then it took an hour to fully dissipate.

Something similar happened on Apollo 13. The S-IVB impacted the Moon 85 miles from Apollo 12's ALSEP—CMP Jack Swigert joked at the time that it was the only thing on that mission to go right. It hit with the force of 11 and a half tons of TNT. This translated to a seismic impact peaked after seven minutes with shockwaves 30 times greater and four times longer than those from Apollo 12's LM impact.

The vibrations from these two impacts lasted longer than scientists expected, far longer than any equivalent vibrations last on Earth. It was almost as if the Moon was ringing like a bell. This strange result forced scientists to think differently about the Moon and its composition.

For an object to ring, it has to be hollow. Following that logic, it would seem that for the moon to ring, it also would have to be hollow, like a bell. When I asked Mou if it was hollow, the answer was:

Yes, the dark side is the entrance.

In a later session I asked another guide, who was not an alien spirit, the same question and he replied:

Not necessarily. There are gases creating density.

"Are you saying there are gas pockets within the moon that give the appearance of it being hollow?"

In other words, yes.

"Does our moon have a gas core?"

Core is solid.

"Are there any entrances that would allow access to the hollow parts of the moon?"

Potentially.

"Are there any extraterrestrials currently with a base on the moon?"

No.

I had read on the Internet a rumor that aliens had actually placed the moon in its present orbit. When I asked Mou if our moon had been artificially placed in its position, he replied:

No, natural moon but it is possible to do on a smaller scale.

"Are there any aliens currently on our moon?"

No.

His answer verified what we had been told by the other guide.

I followed up on something we had been told earlier. "You told us there were aliens present when we sent our astronauts to the moon. Did they all leave?"

Yes.

I guess they decided there was not enough room for both of us.

How Did It Get There?

Our moon is a very interesting structure. While it seems quite large to humans, in reality it is only the fifth largest moon in the solar system. Jupiter lays claim to the largest moon with the one named Ganymede. Ours is thought to date back 4.5 billion years and creates the dynamic movement of the oceans through tides that make life possible on our planet. Earth is considered to be around the same age, so the moon and the Earth were created around the same time.

There are many theories about how the moon was formed, but the one getting the most attention is the giant impact hypothesis. It states that as the young Earth was forming around 4.5 billion years ago, give or take a few years, an object about the size of Mars collided with our planet creating a massive explosion. Either a part of the Earth broke off from our planet or a massive debris field solidified and was captured by the Earth's gravity. There is one flaw to the theory in that the composition of the moon and Earth are chemically identical. The impacting object should have left some of its chemical identity. I thought I would check out the theory with my alien spirit. I started by asking him if he knew how the moon was formed. His answer was:

Yes.

I could almost see him laughing on the other side. He knew damn well that I was looking for the information. I reworded the question to "Would you be kind enough to tell us?"

At your beginning there was a collision.

He was confirming the giant impact hypothesis. I asked if the impact was with another planet.

Yes.

"Was it with a planet we are familiar with?"

No.

"So you are telling us that the particles or debris formed from the collision formed what is now our moon?"

Yes.

Score one for the astronomers on this one, they were correct.

The Red Planet, Mars

Mars, the red planet. Compared in size with Earth. Adobe Stock.

No planet in our solar system gets more attention than Mars. Known as the red planet because its surface is heavy in iron oxide, the planet can be clearly seen by the naked eye. It actually comes relatively close to Earth, 35 million miles, at times in its orbit, making its appearance even more striking. The diameter of Mars is approximately one-third that of Earth, and while our average temperature is around sixty degrees, the average on Mars is a balmy -81 degrees. Gravity is only about one-third of that on Earth and the atmosphere is quite thin, consisting of mostly carbon dioxide. All that being said, it is quite possible that those conditions could be ideal for another alien culture. I started by asking if any aliens currently inhabited Mars.

No.

That answer should stop a lot of rumors. When I inquired if the red planet was ever inhabited, he answered:

Yes.

Although the environment seems a bit inhospitable at the current time, my next question was, "Why did they leave the planet?"

Not of choice.

"Did the planet lose its atmosphere?"

Yes.

"Did Mars ever have oceans?"

Yes, smaller. Lost oceans, then atmosphere.

Mou said that we must be able to travel the stars if we are to survive. It looks like what happened to Mars is a good example of why we need to evolve.

If you observe the surface of Mars, you will find that half of the planet is relatively smooth while the other half is heavily cratered. Our scientists have multiple theories how this happened, but the answer remains a mystery. I asked our guide how this happened.

Storm.

When he gave this answer, I thought about the normal storms of Earth. However, the guide clarified his answer and stated:

No, more a meteor storm.

Apparently, that side of the planet was subjected to a huge storm of meteors. Its thin atmosphere would have provided little protection.

Jupiter

Jupiter is by far the largest planet in our solar system with a radius of 43,441 miles. That means if you were to drill a tunnel from one side to the other, the tunnel would be 86,882 miles long, or it would take light almost one-half-a-second to travel through the tunnel. It is a very interesting planet, possessing at least sixty-seven

Jupiter, the largest planet, with its major moons. Adobe Stock.

moons and a gaseous surface. Compared to Earth, with its density of 5.51 grams per cubic centimeter, Jupiter is not nearly as dense with one of 1.326 grams per cubic centimeter. Scientists attribute this lower density to the gaseous nature of the planet.

While probably having a solid core, there is no well- defined surface to the planet. It is so large, its mass is two-and-one-half the mass of all the other planets in our solar system combined. As large as that seems, our sun is 1,000 times larger than Jupiter. The atmosphere is mostly composed of hydrogen and helium. One of its moons, Ganymede, possesses a diameter larger than the planet Mercury. Another moon of interest is Europa, which is believed to have an ice-covered liquid ocean.

When I asked Mou if there was any extraterrestrial activity on Jupiter under its heavy atmosphere, he replied:

No.

I got a different answer when I inquired if there was any alien activity on the moons of Jupiter.

Yes.

In my earlier book, we were told about a moon of Jupiter where there was a lot of activity. Mou's statement at that time was:

One moon off Jupiter. A place not unlike Earth. It is on the back side. You have to look back at it.

Since Jupiter has sixty-seven moons, his answer did not do a lot to clarify which one of the moons was similar to Earth. In a later session, I asked if there really was a moon on Jupiter that was similar to our planet. He reiterated:

Yes.

Can you tell me which moon you are referring to?

6th.

Is that Europa?

Uncertain what you call it.

I decided to pursue more information about the moons of Jupiter.

Jupiter's Moon, Europa

IO   EUROPA   GANYMEDE   CALLISTO

The four major moons of Jupiter. Adobe Stock.

Did you know that Jupiter has a moon named Europa that is covered in ice, and that ice covers an ocean deep within the planet? The icy surface is assumed to be around 1 1/4 miles (two kilometers) thick, but the ocean is presumed to be water and may reach a depth of about sixty-two miles (one hundred kilometers). It is believed that the water is warmed by the core of Europa, thus creating currents under the ice surface. This moon is considered one of the most likely places to find life in our solar system. When I asked Mou if there was life in the oceans that were on Europa, he replied:

No.

However, I received a different answer when I asked if there was any other type of life on the surface of Europa.

Yes.

"Are you saying there is permanent life on Europa?"

No.

Sometime it is quite exasperating to get a direct answer from my alien buddy. I think he was laughing again. I tried again by inquiring if there were extraterrestrial bases on Jupiter's moon. He answered:

Yes.

We had been told before there was activity on the moons of Jupiter, and he just reaffirmed it. In a later session with another guide, I tried to clarify what was taking place on Europa by asking if he meant that the moon in question was the sixth in size?

From the planet.

We had also been told in the past that there is life on Jupiter. When I asked if that was true, the answer was:

Yes.

Can you describe the life?

Microbile.

That was a term with which I was not familiar. I inquired if that was any type of life form we were familiar with.

Not as you know it.

I was not familiar with the term "microbile" until I read about the discovery of strange life forms in Antarctica and found that NASA has discovered microbial life forms in the depths of Antarctica's Lake Vida, under a sheet of ice sixty-five feet thick. They say these colonies have been prospering in isolation for millions of years and are remnants of life from when the continent was in a warmer climate. Once again, our largest obstacle to learning is the lack of human knowledge. As we continue our space exploration, I predict there will be a wealth of information gained around the planet Jupiter.

Saturn

Saturn, compared to the size of Earth. Adobe Stock.

Whenever we think of Saturn, the most obvious feature is its rings, but it is also quite large with a radius of 36,184 miles. There are nine continuous rings that surround the planet consisting mostly of ice and rock debris. It is a gaseous planet, much like Jupiter, but is ninety-five times larger in mass than Earth. Since it is gaseous in nature, it only is one-eighth as dense as Earth. Our planet has a density of 5.51 grams per cubic centimeter while that of Saturn is 0.687. That means that the planet Saturn is so light that it would actually float in water! There may actually be another reason why Saturn has such a low density. We had been told in the past that the planet was hollow. In a more recent channeling event, I asked our guide if the planet really was hollow and he replied:

Yes.

Saturn with 5 of its largest moons. Adobe Stock.

Another interesting fact is that there are surface winds on the planet that have a maximum strength of 1,118 mph (1,800 kilometers per hour). There are sixty-two known moons that orbit the planet. One of the moons, Titan, is larger than the planet Mercury and is known to have an atmosphere. That moon is said to have an icy crust. Its atmosphere extends nearly 370 miles into space compared to the atmosphere of Earth that extends only thirty-seven miles. Interestingly, the atmosphere consists mostly of hydrocarbons and methane.

Saturn is often referred to as a gas giant because of its low density. When I asked if there was any life on Saturn, the reply was:

Not much but rather around it.

"What happens around Saturn?"

Its life.

With sixty-two moons, I guess it makes sense that there would be more opportunity for life on them than on the planet. The answers concerning the life form were not what I expected. I asked what kind of life and he answered:

Energy beings as best you would know.

Can you describe this type of energy being?

I would be speaking Greek.

My guess is this was a definite slur on my ability to understand. I let the apparent insult slip by without comment and inquired if they have a shape.

They can form.

"Do they ever come to Earth?"

Yes, they travel.

Not only do they travel, they travel long distances. Saturn is 746 million miles from Earth. When I asked if earthlings ever see them, his answer was:

Yes.

"Do they have a defined shape?"

No.

Once again we have been told that there are strange life forms within our planetary system that we have never imagined. Light Beings from Saturn would definitely fall under that category. When I inquired if the Light Beings were considered intelligent life, the answer was:

Yes.

I think one of the biggest surprises earthlings get as we learn to travel the stars will be the number of types of intelligent beings that will be encountered.

Uranus

Uranus, seventh planet from the sun. Adobe Stock.

Uranus, the seventh planet form the sun, is kind of nondescript except for its strange name. In spite of what many people think, the name is derived from the Greek god, Ouranos. It is a fairly large planet with a radius of 15,759 miles. It is similar to Neptune in composition with ice and rock. It has five major moons.

The atmosphere of Uranus is quite complex, consisting mostly of helium and hydrogen. Much of the atmosphere is also water, ammonia, and methane. There seems to be a transition from gas to liquid, and this planet is also known as an ice giant. When photographed, it appears blue, because the methane clouds lay on top of the atmosphere, which absorb the red light, making the blue appearance. The planet has a rocky interior but not a clearly defined interface between the atmosphere and the planets interior, since it consists mostly of ice. Uranus is the coldest atmosphere in our solar system with atmospheric temperatures as low as -370 degrees Fahrenheit.

With all the negative characteristics, when I asked Mou if there was life on Uranus, I expected a negative answer. However, he said:

Yes.

"Are you trying to tell me there is a permanent colony of extraterrestrials on Uranus?"

They come and go.

"Which beings come and go?"

Tintand and Grays.

I had never heard the name Tintand before. In a later session I asked our guide who a Tintand was, he replied:

Not your human life.

I think I already realized that. I pressed him to find out what type of life the guide was referring to.

Light.

"Are you referring to Light Beings?"

Perhaps.

He was certainly not rushing to give us detailed information. When I asked if he could be more specific, the answer was:

They are not of solid matter.

I find it quite hard to comprehend a life form that does not consist of solid matter. At least we are familiar with the grays.

Neptune

The planet Neptune is the eighth planet and is located a long way from the sun. It takes 164.8 years to make a single orbit around the sun. Temperatures on the planet get as low as -360 degrees Fahrenheit, and there are surface winds as fast as 1,300 mph. It is almost seventeen times the mass of Earth with a radius of 15,299 miles. It has a large moon, Triton, as well as fourteen other moons. The

Neptune, eighth planet from the sun. Adobe Stock.

planet has a solid surface and an atmosphere consisting mostly of hydrogen and helium. Its composition is considered to be much like the planet Uranus. It has a blue appearance because of traces of methane in the atmosphere. Its density is 1.638 grams per cubic centimeter, quite light when compared to Earth but heavier than Saturn. Since water weighs 1.0 gram per cubic centimeter, Neptune would sink in a tub of water. This light weight suggests another possibility. We had been told in earlier sessions that several of our planets were hollow. When I asked if Neptune was one of them, the answer was:

Yes.

"Is there currently life on Neptune?"

No.

"Has there ever been life on Neptune?"

Yes.

"What happened to the life that was on Neptune in the past?"

Put to death.

That was definitely not an answer I was expecting. When I asked him if "put to death" was the proper message, he replied:

Yes.

"Were they murdered?"

Yes.

I thought that things were peaceful out there because of the treaty. Mou had told us in earlier sessions there was violence between members of the galactic community before the committee came into existence. I asked if these people were killed before the treaty came into existence and he replied:

Yes.

"Who murdered the beings that used to live on Neptune?"

Duars.

"Is that an alien type?"

Yes.

"Are we familiar with them?"

No.

According to our guides, the lack of life on Neptune is evidence of the once-violent past of our galaxy.

Pluto

Pluto, the farthest planet from the sun. Adobe Stock.

Our ninth body is a dwarf planet having a radius of only 738 miles; it is located the furthest from the sun, approximately 3.7 billion miles. It is quite small, with a width of only 1,400 miles. This is about equal to half the width of the United States. The surface temperature of Pluto can approach -387 degrees F. making the coldest surface temperature. It is composed of two-thirds rock and one-third ice. Because of its small size and distance from the sun, it was only discovered in 1930. Pluto has five moons, one of which is almost one-half the size of the planet.

It is hard for me to comprehend any life form that is capable of surviving in such a cold and inhospitable environment. I was quite surprised when I asked if there was life on Pluto and he replied:

Yes.

When I asked if he could describe the life form, he answered with a single word:

Green.

The first thing that came into my mind was all the jokes about little green men. Maybe the jokes are not as funny as everyone thinks. My follow-up question inquired if he was referring to green people. Apparently, I should not have referred to them as people.

No, your planet is of people, not anywhere else.

When you are conversing with a spirit being from another world, you have to be very specific. I rephrased the question and asked what type of individuals live on Pluto.

Green.

It was becoming apparent this line of questioning was going nowhere. My next questions inquired if the green life form was on any other planet. He replied:

They do not travel.

At least we learned that there really are green beings on other planets. Since they do not travel, we cannot expect to see them show up on Earth. You might find it comforting to know that if you really do see a green alien it is not from Pluto.

The Ninth Planet

Did you know that the axis of the sun is tilted six degrees, and for 150 years scientists have attempted to explain what causes the tilt? I must confess that I had no idea and in addition have no idea why I should care. As it turns out, current studies hypothesize that the tilt may be caused by a large and undiscovered planet outside the orbit of Pluto. This heavenly body is often referred to as Planet X, not to be confused with Nibiru. I asked Mou if there was a ninth, undiscovered planet in our solar system. His reply was:

Yes, trapped.

I assume he meant that it was trapped by the gravitational pull of our sun. I asked if it was beyond Pluto.

Yes.

"Will it ever come close to Earth?"

No.

In a later session with a different guide, I attempted to get additional details about what was in the far reaches of our solar system and asked if there really was another planet beyond Pluto. He answered a little differently.

No, there is a star fragment beyond.

I always thought that all stars emitted light. "Are you saying that it is not a planet but a star fragment that is rotating our sun beyond Pluto?"

Yes, it is burned out, as you could best describe.

Many scientists believe that a burned-out star creates a black hole. My next question inquired if this burned-out star was a black hole.

Not as you know them to be. Remnants.

"Will it ever come close to Earth?"

Not to say.

At least Mou had told us earlier that it would not come close to Earth. It appears our astronomers are correct when they state that there seems to be a large, undiscovered object outside the orbit of Pluto whose gravitational mass is affecting the orbits of the known planets and causing the sun to tilt.

Our own solar system, although miniscule when compared to the size of just our galaxy, is a place of unique mysteries and beauty. Despite what we consider our considerable advances in human abilities to study our local neighborhood in space, we have only cracked the surface of what there is to learn. Hopefully, as humans advance in their knowledge, they will use what they learn for the advancement of our culture. Maybe their first step is to listen to the messages from the spirit world around us.

CHAPTER 3

UNIVERSALITY OF GODS, JESUS, MARY MAGDALENE, AND MORE

You are about to read a very controversial chapter. I am simply passing on information that was given to me by multiple spirit guides, both human and alien. Once again, please keep an open mind and do not shoot the messenger. In this chapter, I will investigate the existence of a supreme deity and other aspects of spirituality from the viewpoint of a very unusual source; the spirit of an alien from a planet far away in our Milky Way. In order for this chapter to be believed, you have to accept the fact that aliens have souls the same as humans. As Mou said, once you open your mind, anything is possible. As you will see, even the most devout believer has underestimated the role played by such a celestial deity.

I will also investigate the role of Jesus as a deity and ask the guides questions concerning his life and death. When the guides are questioned whether he really was the son of God, you will be surprised by the answer. We also investigate the role of master guides and discuss their accomplishments here on Earth. Our guides discuss Jesus, the man, and his relationship with Mary Magdalene.

As mankind has matured to its present state, it has undergone a huge metamorphosis in understanding the form of an all-knowing deity. With thousands of organized religions, it is quite difficult to understand the "true" and correct path to not only believing in but finding the truth about our God. Our own written history concerning God and his son has been corrupted by key gospels being destroyed, gospels being omitted for political purposes, and translators interjecting their own beliefs to the extent that there is no way to actually know the true teachings of Christ. During the Middle Ages, the word of God was preached in Latin to keep the average person from being able to understand what was being spoken.

Since humans have free will, perhaps fifty percent of our population disavows any belief in a supreme being, at least until their time of death approaches. The old saying that "there is no such thing as an atheist in a foxhole" comes to mind. As the end of life draws near, the percentage of non-believers diminishes. As you will see, free will or your choice not to believe, is part of our Galactic God's plan.

If you read my book *Afterlife: What Really Happens on the Other Side*, you know that the guides informed us that the energy of the soul can be neither created nor destroyed; it lasts for eternity. It is my belief that this is the concept of everlasting life referred to in biblical teachings. As my knowledge advanced and we gained the ability to communicate with spirits not of this incarnate dimension, we were told many things that pertained to spiritual existence.

In my book *Aliens Among Us: Exploring Past and Present*, I shared with you that extraterrestrials not only exist but have souls, much the same as humans, even to the extent that they reincarnate to gain soul experience, like humans. It is the existence of this soul that allows us to communicate directly with the souls of extraterrestrials. That is an awful lot of information to absorb, but it is exactly how things work in this incredible Universe.

All Things Past and Future

Mou's knowledge seems to be inexhaustible. One evening I asked him if he could see the future. His answer was quite interesting.

> *I am dead so I see all time because in essence it has already happened.*

I don't pretend to understand all the implications of that statement, but I can vouch that Mou has a knowledge of what will happen in the future as well as what has happened in the past. He has given me this information to try to inform the public about the beneficial intent of our extraterrestrial visitors. The guides also want to inform our civilization that there is a powerful deity that wants all of us to "play nice."

As you will also see, he wants us to understand that all powerful deities exist throughout the Universe and that Heaven is real and has a distinct purpose. When I asked him why he was giving us this information, he replied:

> *This is the continuing of helping people to learn to question everything and if you can think, it can be true.*

I feel sorry for individuals who cannot open their minds to all the incredible possibilities of the happenings in the universe. For instance, during hundreds of years we have been told that the Bible represents the entirety of the teachings of God and his only son, Jesus. This chapter will present some information that should at least present the concept that we may not have been given all the information.

Each Galaxy Has a God

In an early channeling session he certainly stretched the limits of my imagination when he said:

> *Right, now you have to remember that each galaxy has its own God. Each galaxy has its own laws and not all galaxies have the same laws.*

Remember what I said about having to think big? Many people find it hard to believe there is a God that looks after our relatively small planet with a young civilization. Our sun defines our solar system and there are an immense number of suns in our galaxy, the Milky Way. The Milky Way galaxy has more than 100 billion stars. That is one huge congregation for our God! By way of example, imagine our sun as a grain of sand. If each sun in our galaxy represented a grain of sand, there would be enough sand to fill an Olympic-sized swimming pool. Suffice to say, that is really a lot of suns. Now realize that there is one God in charge of all those solar systems and planets. Now you know why I said you would have to think big. He also made another statement that caught my attention and pointed out my obligation to accuracy in this chapter.

> *We need to get this chapter just right.*

I totally agree that when you are talking about something as powerful as the Gods of the Universe, there could be severe repercussions for inaccuracy. You will see that many of words in this chapter are from our alien guide.

In a later session he reiterated the one constant that ties all life together. So there is one fast and sure law. Universally all galaxies have a God. Whether there is life or not, if there is a formed star mass, there is a God, and when there is a God there is life striving to gain enough knowing to understand first that there is a God and what God is all about. On planets in the same galaxy there are many, many life forms seeking understanding of the one God.

It was becoming quite apparent that our alien spirit had a gigantic understanding of what took place in our Universe, both physically and spiritually. When I asked him how he was a source of so much information he replied:

> *Now that I am without form I have studied many Gods and understand.*

It appears that you gain soul experience during an incarnate life but expand your knowledge while not being restricted by a body. When in an incarnate body, you cannot grasp the full expanse of the learning you have experienced in prior lives. When you enter this incarnate life, your prior life memory slate is wiped clean.

A Soul Is a Soul

Not only is there life after death, the soul can study and learn in preparation for the return to another incarnate life. I believe a soul learns on the other side and gains experience through multiple incarnate lives, and your actions create a karma that follows you in future lives. The more I questioned the various aspects of the soul, I began to realize how little I truly understood. One evening I asked him if alien souls are the same as human souls. His answer was not what I expected.

A soul is a soul. A big tree, a dog. Me and you are all one in the end. Souls are the same as me. We can talk about when souls join later.

As we continued to learn more and more about the complexities and composition of souls, both animal and human, I realized that the subject was so complex that it would have to be addressed at a future time, and this book was not the proper venue to fully investigate this subject. I will tackle this subject in depth in the future.

The Concept of Multiple Heavens

If each being on planets with advanced cultures have a soul, the soul must go somewhere when that individual passes. Attempting to follow that logic, I asked if each inhabited planet has a Heaven. His answer brought up a lot more questions.

Each God has a Heaven.

This was starting to get really complicated. It took a little while for the concept of multiple Heavens to sink in. I knew that he was interacting with human spirit guides so I asked what I thought was going to be an obvious answer. "When aliens die, do they go to the same Heaven as humans?"

It depends. Yes, if we are from the Milky Way, we have the same God and thus we go to the same Heaven. If we are from a different God, we go to that Heaven. Heavens are just for the living. Once we progress out of Heaven, we can go anywhere.

Every time I think I am beginning to understand what he is saying, he throws a curve ball. In this case the curve ball was, "Heavens are just for the living." I always thought you had to be dead to go to Heaven. Remember what I said about having to stretch your imagination? I asked him what he meant by that statement. His answer kind of made sense.

That is where we go when staging for life. Coming and going. If you are not in plans for a life, then there are millions of other places to be and to do. It is physical, and most other dimensions are energy, not physical.

This was the first time I ever heard that your soul was only in Heaven when you were preparing to reincarnate, and that if you were not planning to return, your soul was free to travel the galaxy. We were told in earlier channeling sessions by human spirit guides that the soul makes the decision if it wants to return in an incarnate form. I asked Mou if the alien soul makes the decision to come back just like humans.

Just like you, but other Gods have other rules so if you are from other Gods, you do it that God's way. Generally speaking, we are all doing the same growing. Some live 1,000 years so reincarnation is slower because only so many souls can live at a time.

Our planet seems to have a huge population in relation to its size. Since there can only be so many human souls available, I asked him if war is an efficient means of controlling our large world population.

This is one means. There is of course age. You die rather quickly and you are made sick easily. All of this allows many souls on your planet. Other planets like mine are natural, only allows a birth when a death has occurred.

It is an interesting concept that younger cultures are given shorter lifetimes so the ability to screw up is limited for everyone. The way things are going for humans lately, I think there will definitely be a shortening in our average life spans.

Playing by the Rules

"You said different Gods have different rules. Can you give me an example of a rule that is different in another galaxy?"

No, because there are no words to explain it. One God has a total group of feelings that your world, say has never felt. How can you explain that feeling? I cannot explain an emotion you have never felt.

It never occurred to me that there were emotions that were never felt by humans. He also said that once we progress out of Heaven we can go anywhere. I asked him what you have to do to progress out of Heaven.

That means Heaven is a place that once you leave we are free to roam the space continuum.

I am assuming that if your soul is not planning to reincarnate, its soul energy is free to travel around the Universe. In previous sessions, we have interviewed human souls that have made the decision not to reincarnate. They prefer the environment on the other side, free of pain, to coming back to the grief and suffering of an incarnate body.

God Has Many Sons

In an interview that took place during the Christmas season, Mou made a statement that really got my attention.

We have a Christmas-like holiday. Most places do, most all.

The more you communicate with aliens, the more you realize just how many similarities there are when you compare their lives with ours. To have a holiday celebrating the birth of the son of God, he would have had to send his son to other life forms on other planets. I asked him if he was saying that God had a son that was born on other planets.

It is done when the son is born on our planet.

I tried to clarify what he was saying by asking again if he was stating that each intelligent planet had a Jesus or son of God that was sent to them.

Right, we all have our stories on the creation of our species. We all have stories on our one God, and most have stories and holidays on when our wise ones are born and we celebrate our ones who are the ones of God. See, there are always those who teach us of the one God.

Mou was telling us that the birth of our Lord was not a unique event but a miracle that has taken place on other planets that hold intelligent life. I inquired if on his planet he had stories similar to the ones we celebrate at Christmas.

So on my planet we have many stories about the wise ones who were born to help us find our God. Now you all know the story of a man called Christ, the son of God. We call this soul, this son of God, Hegets. He was born on my planet too, as were a few others, but because it is his time, we will only talk of him. On my planet, a male is born and this man is sent by God to bring religion equality where no matter who you are you can pray in his house and no matter what sex, you can speak his words. In my time he had come and gone 4,000 years.

Notice he said there were others sent during earlier times. If there were multiple sons of God sent to Robbe, I wondered if there were multiple sons sent to Earth. When I asked him if there were sons of God sent to our planet other than Jesus, the reply was:

Yes.

"How many?"

Beginning with humans, eight.

"Can you name them for me?"

Moses, Abraham, Jesus, Vocur.

His list was including the founding fathers of our religions. Vocur was a name I had never heard before. I asked him how many years before the birth of Christ that God sent this son. His answer was:

5,000 years.

"Was he Egyptian?"

No.

"Was he born in Mesopotamia?"

Yes.

If God sent his son to the Sumerians as a teacher, that would certainly help explain their rapid advancement.

Son of God on Mou's Planet

It seems like 4,000 years is a long time ago, but on his planet where individuals live around 1,000 years this was only four generations. I thought I would clarify by asking if he was saying that their son of God was born 4,000 years before his time.

> *He is still teaching us to play nice. OK, so on my planet he dies an old man and we celebrate his leaving us and we get together to sing and pray and thank him for his wisdom. To you we say it is a great man you celebrate. My planet we use this time like you do at Thanksgiving. We sit down to dinner [absorbing minerals] with family and say why we are happy. We give a gift of love to each other, and if we are thinking of marriage, this is the day that we declare it. So, see, kind of the same.*

I found the similarity in the celebration of the birth of the son of God on our two planets so many light years apart to be amazing. He had described himself in life as standing over nine feet and having bluish skin. In my mind I can see his family sitting around a large table celebrating the birth of their son of God. I wonder if they dine on turkey and stuffing or just sit there and ingest their minerals?

On Earth, God gave us the free will to believe in him or not. I asked him if there were any non-believers on his planet.

Many. Like your planet, God is all around yet there are those who say it is not so, that there is nothing after life.

The similarities between our two cultures is absolutely amazing! God has given universal free will throughout our galaxy and even among advanced cultures individuals are free to deny his presence.

I was intrigued by the fact that he said each galaxy has its' own God. When I asked if there was one overall Supreme Being that controlled the Universe, he replied:

It is like a pyramid. You start out with many. Everyone has someone over them. They are independent but interdependent. Until you work yourself up and up until there are three. Those three gods watch over us all. These Gods change from time to time. As a God works themselves up to that level. The thinking being that any soul can be a God if willing.

See what I mean about having to think big?

Who Really Was Jesus?

Very few readers will enter this section of the book with an open mind. The Bible clearly tells us that he was the son of God born to us more than 2,000 years ago, a great teacher that was crucified and resurrected to join his father in Heaven. Upon his death his disciples spread the word of teachings to ultimately make him one of the greatest prophets to ever walk the Earth. One night I asked our guide if Jesus was the son of God. He replied:

Yes, as you all are.

I had never really thought about the origin of our individual souls. Once again the guide had ducked my question.

All are sons. Each of you. You are all of God.

One thing I have realized from many years of channeling is that sometimes it is nearly impossible to get a guide to directly answer a question. This was one of those times. Changing the subject, I inquired if the soul of Jesus has ever reincarnated.

No.

"Will the soul of Jesus ever return in the future?"

No.

"Is the story of the resurrection that appears in the Bible accurate?"

Yes.

Where our son of God was crucified, the son of God on the planet Robbe died of old age. My guess is death by crucifixion is the result of our civilization at the time being quite violent while the inhabitants of Mou's planet had gotten over the violence thing by that time.

The Gospel Fix Was In

Roman Emperor Constantine selected the gospels for the Bible. Adobe Stock.

Even the creation of the New Testament of the Bible failed to provide true information and reflected the political needs of the Roman Emperor Constantine. According to documents of the era, it is interesting to note that the selected gospels that were to become the New Testament were agreed upon by unanimous vote. Constantine threatened to exile anyone that disagreed. Official Christianity got off to a very Democratic start as the Nicene Creed became the official doctrine! Constantine even declared himself "the vice regent of God," whatever that meant. When the gospels were selected by Constantine at the Nicaea Conference in 325 AD, more gospels were rejected than accepted for his political expediency. Unfortunately, some of the most important gospels, such as that of Mary Magdalene and Jesus himself, were rejected. We are told that Jesus taught and wrote of reincarnation and an alien presence. The Emperor decided that the writings of the greatest teacher of all times were not suitable to be taught to the masses. Constantine guaranteed that the first Bible was a collection of verses that solidified his political position, not to give a true interpretation of the teaching of the son of God.

Pope Sylvester I. He helped select the books of the Bible. Adobe Stock.

In an earlier session, we had the honor of channeling with Pope Sylvester I, who was the Pope of the Catholic Church from 314 to 345 AD, the time period when Constantine selected the gospels to be used in the Bible. I asked the Pope if there were gospels that were presented that were omitted. He replied:

There were many gospels missing.

"Did you know Constantine?"

I did.

"Did Constantine discuss with you what books were to be omitted?"

I was conferred with.

"Why were some of the gospels omitted?"

I was not in agreement with all.

"Did Constantine make the final decision as to what books were omitted?"

Yes.

"What was the primary gospel that was left out of the Bible?"

Teachings of Jesus.

"Why were the gospels omitted?"

There were fears.

"What were some of the teachings of Jesus that were omitted?"

Reincarnation; it was always in the obvious.

According to the spirits themselves, the Bible is a historical document that has been influenced by man and their politics throughout the ages. Perhaps the best example occurs in the omitted Gospel of Mary Magdalene.

Gospel of Mary Magdalene

The female disciple Mary Magdalene. Adobe Stock.

The rejected and subsequently lost gospels have always intrigued me, especially the gospel of Mary Magdalene. We do know from the Bible that Mary was present at the crucifixion and the resurrection. Her gospel indicates that she was also a favored disciple and possibly very close to Jesus. I asked the guide how she became a disciple of Jesus.

Same as the others, followed.

"Why was her gospel not accepted by Constantine to become a book of the Bible?"

She was a woman.

"Can you tell me what teachings were included in her gospel?"

Witness to the teachings of the great teacher.

"Was Mary the favorite disciple of Jesus?"

Nurtured her differently. Was her protector.

"Was Mary ever a prostitute?"

Not in your modern terms.

Out of respect, I decided not to continue this line of questioning, so I asked if Jesus had a personal relationship with Mary. He replied:

Yes.

"Were they married?"

Not as you are married.

At the time of Jesus, marriages were not the formal event they are today. I continued by asking, "Were they soul mates?"

You could say that, yes.

"Was Mary present at the crucifixion of Jesus?"

Both Marys, yes.

The guides were being quite helpful in explaining what the truth is surrounding the life of Mary and Jesus. Next, I asked what was considered the most important teaching of Jesus.

Love. If there is love, there is everything.

In a session several years ago with Saint Timothy, I had asked what it was like to know Jesus and he replied:

To know Jesus, was to know pure love.

This seems to be the universal message and the key to our advancing to join the rest of the galactic community. Maybe the key to us advancing is to eliminate political parties.

Guides and Master Guides

There are spirit guides that help lead us through our ordinary lives. By assisting humans, the spirits also learn and in turn advance their standing and level on the other side. A master guide has advanced to the highest level and is approaching a oneness with God. There are times when these master guides decide to return to Earth in an attempt to assist the struggling human race. In order to become a Master, the spirit must spend lifetimes on other planets as part of their learning experiences and to understand different emotions not felt on our planet. As I was to find out, returned master guides have played a huge role in our development. I feel that in order to understand the role of God in our galaxy, it is important to understand his closest helpers, the Master guides. I inquired if there were many that returned to Earth.

Many, many.

"Were any of our presidents in that category?"

No.

"Were many of them religious figures?"

Some.

"Can you name a few?"

Jesus.

"I thought he was the son of God?"

Master.

"Are you saying he was a Master guide and not the son of God?"

You are all sons of God.

No matter how I rephrase the question, this is always the answer.

Master Guides Returned

"If all of us are sons of God, what made Jesus different?"

He was a great teacher whose job was to change mankind, as if you will.

"Was Mahatma Gandhi a returned Master? "

Yes.

"If Gandhi was a returned Master, can you name any more like him?"

Great teachers, many. Masters are simply souls more experienced but not more or less than you or I. We are very much the same over here as you might say. That is your term not ours.

I could not resist asking what he meant by the "your term" statement.

We do not term them anything. We are one. Humans are great storytellers.

An overriding theme over there seems to be the equality and oneness of souls, and they only differ as to their experiences of learning. My next question was, "Will you give me the name of another returned master guide?"

Teresa, highly evolved.

That got Connie's attention: Mother Teresa is one of her guides and spiritual advisors. I stated that Billy Graham is a great teacher and asked if he is a returned Master.

Do not confuse Master for ascended, to use your language.

"How would you refer to them in your language?"

Many great teachers have come.

"What determines that a Master guide is returned to Earth?"

That soul.

So the master guides observe the humans making a mess of things and make their own decision when they feel they are required to return and give a hand. My next question was, "Were there any other Master guides, like Jesus, that were sent to Earth?"

Many.

I wish I would have thought to ask what it was that separated Jesus from the many other Master guides. Our guides in various sessions have attempted to explain just how far-reaching the power of our God is. Not only does he send Masters to us in an attempt to advance our souls, but he conducts similar guidance to all the other planets in our galaxy that contain intelligent life, much of it far more intelligent than ours. I guess there is hope that eventually our planet will advance to the level of the others and we all realize that not violence but love and kindness will allow us to join the civilized universe. In my final question to the guides, I asked if God sent any other of his sons to Earth. He replied:

You are all of God.

There is that answer again! Different guides will give somewhat different answers, but the underlying concept of their answers are the same.

Free Will for All

We have repeatedly seen that an overriding rule of the galaxy is free will for the souls, be they on Earth, Heaven, or other planets. At times I will ask questions about future events that they will refuse to answer, because answers will create negative energies that hinder soul learning. For instance, one night I asked who the guides would like to see elected as our next president. His answer was not what I expected.

> *To us it is unimportant as it is not our area of experience. You chose to have this experience.*

I think he was telling us that we were creating our own negativity over the current presidential campaign and it was not helping anyone's soul advance. That opinion was reinforced one night when I attempted to get a future prediction by asking what event will cause the next large loss of life in the United States. His answer included a bit of a reprimand.

> *Now Barry, why do you ask such things? Each day is a new set of probabilities. If you could have such powers, then you would have no need to ask. You seek knowing. Such things distract one's journey. It is all much grander than you allow yourself to understand. You have come to learn.*

I have learned when they begin an answer with "Now Barry," it is time to change the subject. Even guides can be a little short of patience with humans. I am apparently on a karmic journey, and they will not provide any information that will interfere with that journey. As I found out, they also will not give any information that will financially make my journey any easier. I asked if it would be possible to get a lottery number the other night. The guide replied:

> *1, 2, 3, 4, 5, 6 ,7, 8, 9. Ha, ha, ha.*

Another dream was dashed upon the rocks of reality. This chapter provided a lot of information concerning the beliefs of different cultures in our galaxy concerning the existence and belief in a Deity. Not only do all the advanced cultures of the Milky Way worship the same God, he has sent his son to them in the same way he sent Jesus to Earth. In addition, he has sent other great teachers that have helped us to progress and evolve. It is equally interesting to understand that even in the advanced cultures, there are non-believers. We have also been shown how our own religious beliefs have been influenced and molded by human influences. The more we learn, the more insight we have into the miracle of the universality of a God. We need to take comfort in the knowledge that we are all of God.

REINCARNATION

Past, Present, and throughout the Galaxy

In this chapter we are going to take a unique look at reincarnation. Not only are we going to look at whether it exists and the religious history of its teachings here on Earth, but we are going to look at its existence throughout the galaxy. I have no doubt that if you are still having a hard time believing aliens exist, you are going to have a very hard time believing some of the other information provided herein. Open your minds and I think you will enjoy the trip.

Reincarnation: If at First You Don't Succeed . . .

Reincarnation is defined as the soul energy having everlasting life and being reborn in multiple incarnate lifetimes. I believe that reincarnation is the mechanism by which your soul follows a path in pursuit of an individual's karma and the learning experiences needed to advance your soul energy to higher realms on the other side. As you will learn, the soul's journey takes a far longer time than you ever imagined. The journey of the soul is complicated by the interaction of free will and ego to the point that a single lifetime can pale into insignificance and your ego can create negativity that can negate multiple prior lives.

Hinduism believes that the human spirit comes back in many different forms as it strives for perfection. Other Eastern religions share variations of the concept. More than 1.3 billion Hindus on this planet believe that the soul returns in one form or another after incarnate death. With that many people believing in reoccurring lifetimes, you have to at least accept the possibility of reincarnation.

For my part, I have no doubt of the existence of reincarnation. Through my channeling sessions both Connie and I have gained knowledge of our prior lives and have seen multiple examples of evidence to reinforce our information. One evening I asked Mou if there were any planets where reincarnation did not happen. His reply was pretty emphatic.

Nope. It is a law. Like gravity, you will come back. If you find yourself in a body it is a fact that you have "lifed" and will life again.

Reincarnation was taught long before the birth of Christ throughout the ancient world. Greek philosophers, such as mathematician Pythagoras and Plato, taught aspects of the soul reappearing in various forms. Plato in particular was a proponent in the repeated reappearance of the soul.

Reincarnation and the Gnostic Gospels

The birth and death of Jesus, the great religious teacher that lived 2,000 years ago, brought about multiple schools of thought concerning the soul's journey after death. It all started when Jesus commanded his disciples to spread his teachings to all the world. Unfortunately, he did not direct the apostles which of his teachings he wanted to become the foundation of the Christian Church. Reincarnation was spoken of in private by Jesus but not as part of his public teachings.

The Gnostic school of Christianity taught that the soul was everlasting and would return after death to reincarnate and pursue knowledge and experience until obtaining a oneness with God. The Roman Catholic Church believed that the soul would be judged by its actions during life and ascend to Heaven or spend eternity in Hell. You only got one chance to get it right.

Gnostic Gospels of Thomas, Mary Magdalene, Peter, and others actually taught of reincarnation among many other subjects thought not suitable for what was to become the Catholic Church, an institution ruled predominately by men. Gnostic text spoke of Mary Magdalene being the favorite among the Apostles and hinted at a personal relationship with Jesus. Beliefs such as the virgin birth and resurrection of the body were also questioned. Such teachings were called heresy by the male rulers of the other wing of the church who argued for the banning of such nonsense.

By the time of Emperor Constantine during the beginning of the fourth century and despite persecution by the Romans, the Christian Church was growing in strength, even though divided in what practitioners considered the true teaching of Jesus. At the First Council of Nicaea, held in 325 AD, the Gnostic gospels were rejected as the framework for Christianity. With the rejection of the Gnostic gospels, reincarnation was also officially determined not to be a true teaching.

The Bible, a Political Decision

By 385 AD, any form of Christian teachings that differed with the Nicene Creed was pronounced as heretical, and anyone found to be teaching anything other than that of the Catholic Church would be put to death. No wonder reincarnation was forgotten as a religious teaching for many centuries.

In spite of all the efforts of the church to keep the truth from the people as to the true teachings of Jesus, one verse in the New Testament indicates that there was more to the true meaning of the gospels than survived in the Bible.

He [Jesus] told them, "The secret of the kingdom of God has been given to you. But to those on the outside everything is said in parables so that, they may be ever seeing but never perceiving, and ever hearing but never understanding; otherwise they might turn and be forgiven!"

Mark 4:11–12

The Roman Catholic Church Takes Over

The Roman Catholic Church became the custodian of the "true" gospels and began a campaign to eliminate the teaching that the human soul could return to another incarnate life. Organized religion became a decree that you either believe what is laid out in the Bible or you don't believe at all, and as punishment, you will then rot in Hell for eternity. Where Jesus preached love, teachings of the new Orthodox Church taught that dissent was heresy and all the penalties that went with it. The Church itself was put in the unique position of deciding who the "true" believers were.

By the middle of the sixth century, Roman Emperor Justinian proclaimed that the belief in reincarnation was punishable by death. In addition, Gnostic gospels were to be destroyed. Perhaps the thought of being burned at the stake by the Church was quite a deterrent to believing anything contrary to the selected gospels—which by this time were only translated in Latin, and common people could not read. Through the ages, the thought of leading multiple lifetimes and gaining soul experience faded from memory in Christian religions.

It was not until 1870, with the discovery of the Gospel of the Nazirenes, 1896, with the Gospel of Mary Magdalene, and in 1945, when more of the lost gospels were discovered in northern Egypt that the content of the lost, ancient teachings became public knowledge. Known as the Nag Hammadi Library, this major discovery in 1945, included thirteen ancient codices that contained more than fifty texts including the Gospel of Thomas and the Gospel of Peter, all writings that were considered previously destroyed. Unfortunately, there was considerable damage to the writings, and large portions of the gospels are still missing, probably lost forever.

Early Gospels Teach Reincarnation

Perhaps the lost codex that best refers to reincarnation is the Gospel of the Nazirenes. Early Church fathers believed that there was a collective gospel written by the actual twelve apostles during the period after the death of Jesus. Some scholars believe that the Gospel of the Nazirenes is that collective gospel. There are many instances where the rebirth of the soul is universally written about in this gospel.

As in Adam, all are bound to cycles of rebirth, so in the Lord shall all be made eternal. Blessed are those who are made perfect . . . for . . . their works do follow them.
 —Nazirenes 69:2
 (www.bibliotecapleyades.net)

Aliens and Reincarnation

In the very first session I ever had with Mou in September of 2014, I asked him if aliens reincarnate. He answered:

Just like you, yes.

In a single statement he not only verified that humans reincarnate but that extraterrestrials also have souls that come back for multiple lifetimes. We were getting off to a really good start! In our various channeling sessions since that time, we have been told that the individual soul exercises free will and makes its own decision on when to come back to another incarnate lifetime. When asked about this, his answer was:

Just like you. We all do the same growing.

It was good to know that inhabitants on other planets were also not perfect and had to grow in spiritual stature, same as earthlings. When I asked the purpose of reincarnation the answer was:

Soul experience.

That is exactly the same answer we received from the spirits of Saints here on Earth.

Those Who Have Mastered Life

I asked him the process when a soul decides to reincarnate. You will note that on his planet he uses the term "to life" when referring to the return of the soul to an incarnate lifetime.

There are a million reasons to want to life and twice as many ways to go about it. Like, say one way is you die a very traumatic death? The soul is in shock, so the Masters decide he will be reincarnated fast. The soul goes right to sleep, no greeting time. Then a baby is found and, zap, he has a new life. This makes it easier on the soul. Have a nice life and the bad-ending life is just a memory that the soul deals with later.

He mentioned that your life plan is reviewed by the Masters. We had many sessions with Master guides in the past but this was a new term to me, so I inquired who the Masters were.

> *There are souls here who have mastered life, so these souls stay around to help you with your plans. They gently guide you to a life that flows. Do not have too much to do. One that you can succeed in. Just another loving soul here to help.*

He made another statement that truly indicated the power of the Master guides.

> *It is a new fact, and we want to make sure we include all the facts. Like a Master soul can be both for one planet only or the Master can be like God, universal.*

I always thought God was universal, but I had not heard that a Master guide could be like the Universal God. He went on to clarify when I asked him how a Master soul could be like God, universal. His answer was:

> *He mastered the learning needed to move to the God level. Each soul will grow back to God.*

I asked him what the process was when a soul decides to come back to an incarnate life.

> *For a normal incarnation the soul puts his name on the list. He finds a mom and dad who meets his needs. Then he designs his body, chooses a birth date and time, and with help, he sets his karma up. He decides what he wants to learn to focus on, and then he puts his plans to the Masters who goes over it and sends it back to him either ok or needs work. When he gets this life plan approved, he waits for his body. The soul can come and go in the baby until it is born. Some are always in it while others only go into the baby. And then you are born.*

It seemed like an awful lot of planning went into your life plan before you ever set foot on Earth. I asked just what goes into your life plan.

> *OK. Life is a matter of vast planning on your part and a roll of the dice on the karmas part. We spend a lot of time planning our life. We worry about everything. We spend time making sure everything fits into place. We check, we double and triple check, and then we hand it over to our personal guides, the finders of God, to make sure everything happens and when it should.*

I had no idea that so much planning went into your life plan while on the other side. It seems like every move in your incarnate life is pre-planned. My next question inquired just how efficient all that planning was after you were launched on your incarnate life. Once again the answer was not exactly what I expected.

> *And then life takes hold of it and shreds it to pieces. You have to remember Mother Nature does not have karma. She does how she pleases. Then there are accidents. And then there are Master guides over things and a hundred other things that can go right and wrong. And then there are things like love, free will, and miracles that can change things. About the only thing you can count on is you are born on time.*

Did you ever wonder if God had second doubts about the free will thing? We have been told before that the spirits on the other side consider death the beginning, where humans consider death the end. In the past, we have heard spirits say it was their time when they passed. Many plan their exact time of death into their life plan. I asked Mou if how you die is also predetermined.

> *That part of dying is not a for-sure thing.*

From our previous channeling experiences, we have learned that there is a wide variance in how long it takes a spirit to return. When I inquired if there was any rush to reincarnate, the answer was:

> *Only if you have left things hanging. A soul after death goes through a time of adjustment. When you die you do not magically remember things. Like a soul going into life, you have to adjust to changes. In life it is taken care of, this adjustment time, by being a baby. And in death you are allowed this adjustment time. Many souls that come over panic to rush back. Most of the time their Master guide overrides the request, but if it is important, the soul can go back quickly in a number of ways. Most souls take their time.*

Universal Reincarnation, the Ultimate Goal

I have always wondered what incentive the soul had to keep coming to an incarnate life that guaranteed grief and suffering. When I asked him to define the ultimate goal for a soul he answered:

> *To grow back to God.*

He went on to clarify what he meant by that statement.

> *Be so knowing that you are equal to your God and become a part of him again and maybe have an opportunity to be a god and see how you do. It goes on and on and on. Your God was like us, looking for the key to it all.*

That sounded like an awful lot of learning! I had to see how many lifetimes it took to achieve that level of knowledge.

As many as you need. A billion is a modest number.

I hope he was kidding about the modest number thing. As you move along planning your lives, I wondered if there was any way you could gauge how you were doing as you kept coming back for lives during eons of time. When I asked if there was any way to know how many more lifetimes were required, he answered with a warning.

Note! You never count your eggs until they hatch and that goes for lives. There is a thing called free will and a thing called ego. You may be one life away from perfection, and in that last life your ego runs away with your free will, and when you return, it has made a hundred new karmas and lives. So you see, you are done when you are done.

Once again we were warned that the combination of ego and free will can be like fire and gasoline. The idea that a soul is a soul brought up a very interesting question. I asked if it was possible for a soul to reincarnate in another form, like that of an alien.

Sure. If you stay in your own galaxy. It is done all the time.

I was having a hard enough time getting my head around the fact that a soul could reincarnate as an extraterrestrial, let alone that it would be easy if you stayed in your own galaxy. Maybe I have a narrow point of view, but I was having a problem trying to understand why anyone would want to reincarnate on another planet. While Earth is certainly not perfect, you have to admit there is a lot to learn here. I asked Mou why anyone would want to reincarnate on other planets. He replied:

See, there are a lot of things you cannot know if you only life on one planet. There are hundreds of planes to life on as well as different planets and dimensions. You cannot master feelings until you master life on every place you can life on. Each place has their own set of feelings.

There are certainly a lot of feelings here on Earth. I asked him why mastering the feelings here on Earth were not sufficient.

Here on Earth, energy is hard matter of fact while on my planet they are softer and flexible. There are thousands of feelings you do not and cannot feel in your body or mind.

The idea that you have to master thousands of feelings before your soul is able to meet its full potential is a bit overwhelming. If your soul is to advance, you have to reincarnate on the other planets so you can understand their emotions. No wonder soul advancement is such a long process. I asked him if he ever considered reincarnating as a human. His answer really caught me off guard.

I have been back to life many times and you have lifed many times on mine.

If I am understanding him correctly, he just let me know that my soul had an incarnate life on his planet in the past. Maybe this is why I have been chosen to receive this information. Mou and I might be related in past lives. I asked him if he had ever had an incarnate life on Earth. His reply was:

Yes.

When I asked Mou if he had been on Earth more than 10,000 years ago his answer was also:

Yes.

Maybe he was one of the guys painting in caves in ancient times.

Your Book of Life

On another evening during a board channeling session, I was inquiring into my personal past lives. Our guide for the evening informed me that I had failed to make up-to-date entries in my book of life and when I got back over there I needed to get it up-to-date. She also went on to say that she was not reading about my lives but viewing it. At the time, I did not follow up for more information.

As I became more involved with our alien guide, I thought I would ask him to verify if each soul had a book of life. He filled in more of the details.

If you have lifed, you have a book of life. In this book is written all things. Who you lifed with, who you want to life with again, your relationships, what you learned from them in future lives, who harmed you, who you harmed, who loved you, your favorite things, and what you did not like. The book of life is a reminder of things you will do in upcoming lives. It is a marvelous thing.

In my mind I had a vision of this huge volume being kept in a library in Heaven. I asked him who is responsible for keeping your book of life. He replied:

You are responsible. It is part of your brain you do not use. You take it to every life and it is with you recording your life as it happened, and the hardest part you have to fill in when you come back, and that is why you reacted to things that happened. Your feelings while things went down.

So much for the library idea. I knew we did not use our brains to the fullest, but I never thought you could hide a book there. Our earlier guide had mentioned that she could actually see my past lives in the book. My next inquiry was if he could actually see my prior lives by observing my book.

Out of the top of everyone's head is a thread of energy. It all goes up and connects, so if you know how, I can pick up your thread and read you. It is easy here, harder there. It is like all the wires meeting at the phone company.

I heard the old saying that your life was an open book, but his last statement gave it a whole new perspective. If the information is really in your own mind, I can see how prior life regression through hypnosis is possible. The information is there, you just have to reach for it.

Multiple Choices

Apparently when you are on the other side, your free will lets you make a lot of choices concerning your future lives. We had discussed this in many other sessions, but I thought it would be interesting to investigate those choices by asking a spirit with an alien lifetime in his recent past. My first question inquired if you can pick your relationship with another soul on the other side. He replied:

This is what it is all about. Finding those souls you life with and those you do not. You cannot find out who you want to life with or not to life with if you do not life with them. Life is completely up to you. There is always a loophole.

You have to spend time with a soul in a lifetime to see if you want to spend another one with them. My guess is a loophole is similar to a divorce, only this is for an eternity. Connie and I have been told we have been together for five or six lifetimes. I guess neither of us have bothered to look for a loophole. One of the great mysteries is how two souls decide to get together on the other side, are born, lead separate lives, and know when they just happen to bump into each other. My next question asked, if you pick a soul to marry, how do you know you will find them in life? He had to think about his answer.

How to explain this? Life is a work of art. You sit down at a blank canvas and begin to create. First your personality and your body. From this you pick up parents, siblings. How you want your childhood to mold you. But karma is drawn in a mold. If you have karma with others, that part of the picture is drawn the same. You draw the drive-in where you are going to meet your soul mate. Both have drawn the same event, so when you are lifeing, you are following your work of art, like a road map. You both know you are going and when you get there because both are there and the karma begins.

The more we talked about reincarnation, the more Mou talked about karma, the more I realized that reincarnation and karma were interconnected. Your karma seemed to be such a long-term plan that I thought I would ask if you can plan multiple lifetimes in advance as you seek whatever it is you are looking for. He replied:

> *Most do. You always leave your future life plans open so you can add or take out parts. Some plan 10 lifes ahead while others like flying by the seat of their pants. Personal preference.*

Whenever we have channeled with spirits that passed unexpectedly, they always say it was their time. I asked if there were multiple choices concerning your time of death or was your time precisely chosen before you enter your incarnate life? His answer was:

> *You can do either. You can plan it right down to the millisecond or you can leave it open to when the body finally forces you out. Depends on the soul's wishes.*

"Can a soul request a specific set of parents?"

> *Yes, it does in fact select.*

"How do you know when your soul no longer has to return to continue the learning process?"

> *You cannot know in this state. You'll know.*

When you return to a life state, your memory of past lives is wiped clean. Each lifetime represents a new learning opportunity and karma. I was wondering if your soul only advances when your soul is with body. I asked if your soul can advance when it is on the other side.

> *Yes, learning as a guide.*

"Can you tell me how many future lives my soul will require?"

> *That is not for me to know.*

It is probably better for me not to know the answer to that question. Hopefully not another billion lifetimes.

How about Animals?

Connie and I have just gone through an amazing couple of years where we channeled with our cat that we lost in 2008, and followed him through the reincarnation process. He predicted the date of his return as a black kitten and he found us within one week of the time he predicted. At the time of me writing this chapter, he is eight months old and exhibits many of the characteristics he had in prior life with one exception; in this lifetime he is a female. I thought I would investigate how human and animal souls interact. I started off by asking if there was much difference between human and animal souls.

No.

"Is an animal soul immortal like that of a human?"

Yes.

I knew from previous sessions that we have an animal soul family in much the same way we all have a family of human souls that return through multiple lifetimes. My next question inquired if animals reincarnate outside of their soul family.

No. They arrive for a different experience.

"Are you saying that animal souls advance as do humans during different incarnate experiences?

If they choose. They do not have to.

"Can a human reincarnate as an animal?"

Yes.

"Can an animal reincarnate as a human?"

Yes.

I had a hard time thinking an animal could come back and live the life of a human. In an attempt to clarify, I asked if the guide was telling us that our cat could come back as a human.

If it were so needed.

After that answer, I made a mental note to be extra nice to our cats. I did not want them coming back as a human and kicking my butt. As this session progressed, I began to wonder if there were any limits to the reincarnation of a soul. I inquired if it were possible to return as a tree.

No, but it can have a shared experience.

"Are you telling me a tree has a soul?"

It has an energy source.

"What other forms can be assumed by a human soul?"

Energy can form from the smallest of sources.

There are times when I realize that the information being given by the guides is exceeding my ability to comprehend. The concept of me sharing experiences with a tree was definitely one of those times.

A Harsh but Well-Deserved Judgment

The concept of good and evil permeates the entire galaxy. I have pursued it in various sessions and still have questions on how an individual or group can create such evil deeds here on Earth. One evening I asked a Master guide if there was such a thing as an evil life plan on the other side. His answer was:

Evil is not created over here.

While that was a good answer for humans, I wondered if it held up on other planets. In my mind, the personification of evil is Adolf Hitler. Under his orders, millions of people were sent to their deaths. I thought I would ask Mou if he had planned his life while on the other side.

Now in life you have karma and with this come free will and ego. He set out with good intentions but free will and ego got way out of balance. It was not supposed to happen that way, but once a soul is sent and karma is set it must be played out.

That free will thing really gets a lot of people in trouble. I asked what penalty, if any, he had to pay for what he did while in his last incarnate life. His answer certainly should give everyone pause for thought.

Hitler now has to make whole every soul he affected. His karma from this one life will last many, many lives long. He must do whatever it takes for each soul to forgive him. Think about that. What a learning time he has ahead of him. Note to self, watch your ego.

According to Mou, Adolf is going to be one busy person for a very long time. I am hoping that these "watch your ego" statements are not directed only at yours truly.

A Final Chapter Thought

In this chapter, we have covered the entire spectrum of statements concerning reincarnation. It should now be becoming more apparent the enormity of the soul's journey in attempting to reach the perfection required to be like God. As we concluded the session where I intended to end the questioning on the subject, my final question inquired if Mou had anything else that he wanted to add to the chapter. Once again his words were direct and to the point.

Just because you may not believe in it does not mean it is not true. A thing about stubborn earthlings is if they do not believe in it, it means it is not so. The Earth is still round. Karma happens, end of chapter.

CHAPTER 5

TYPES OF ALIENS AMONG US

W hen I started this chapter on alien types, my belief was that it would be one of the easier chapters to write. In my wildest dreams, I did not believe some of the information about the different extraterrestrial beings would contain such amazing information. Once again, approach this chapter with a very open mind; you are going to need it. I started by asking Mou how many alien types were currently on Earth. He answered:

7 or 8.

Keep in mind there are a huge number of other alien types that are not present on Earth at the current time. From what we have learned, they come and go on a regular basis, so it would be quite difficult to have an up-to-date head count. If you were to believe some of the websites on the Internet, you would think there are a huge number of beings from other planets. I started to name some alien types I had read about and asked if they were present at the current time on our planet.

Alien Presence or Not

"Are Reptilians a valid alien type, and are they currently present on Earth?"

Yes.

"How about Arcturians? "

Yes.

"Pleiadians? "

Yes.

Nordics are supposed to be almost like humans, standing tall with blond hair. When I asked if they were a valid type, his answer was:

Yes.

According to the Internet, some of the fiercest looking beings from other planets are Alpha Draconians. His answer concerning their existence was:

No.

So much for acquiring information from the Internet. Syrian Hybrids?

Yes.

This might have seemed like a stupid question since I am basing a lot of the information in this book from channeling the spirit of a blue alien, but I inquired anyway. Are there blue aliens currently present on our planet?

Yes.

Zetas get a lot of attention. There is even a website called "Zeta Talk." When I inquired if there were Zeta's currently on our planet, he replied:

Yes.

Probably the being type that gets the most attention is the Grays. It would be a severe disappointment if they were not on Earth. When I asked if they were present, the answer was:

Yes.

If you've read my previous alien book, you saw that the image of a spider in the Nazca Lines of Peru was the shape of the aliens that were present. A question about the presence of Spider People was met with:

No.

I was really hoping for a negative answer concerning the spider people. How about the Little Whites?

Yes.

Keep in mind that just because they are not currently active on Earth does not mean they do not exist. I am sure there are others, but at the time I could not think of the names of any more. I did ask him if there were more aliens visiting our planet than in the past, and he replied:

Yes.

I guess that makes sense; humans are messing up so much now there has to be a lot to observe.

The Grays

If you ask the average person to name a type of extraterrestrial, the odds are pretty good they would say "the Grays." If you watch the movies, you will probably think that all grays are evil. When I asked Mou what comprised the mission of the grays here on Earth, he answered:

Stabilizing influences. Both to the Earth and its people.

"How long have they been on our planet, and what is the historic influence of the grays on Earth?"

The iron age, times of discovering mineral and structural growth.

The iron age began around 1,300 BC so they have been here for quite a while. Next, I asked the location of their home planet.

Tepplinow, but it is dead now.

"Are you telling me the home planet of the grays has died?"

Yes.

"What planet do they come from now?"

Home, Ha ha ha ha.

I don't know if they have standup comedy on the other side, but Mou would certainly qualify for a comedy club in Heaven. I thought I would try again and asked him the name of the planet that was currently home for the grays.

They call it Hipvot.

Not a planet I ever heard of. Where is this planet located?

In the middle of the pinwheel.

When I researched the Pinwheel Galaxy I found it to be in the Ursa Major constellation approximately 21 million light years from Earth. They have definitely traveled a long distance to get to Earth. I asked Mou how long they had been located there. He replied:

Many generations.

I thought I would move on and try to get a physical description of them. I started by asking how tall they stood.

Depends on gravity.

Did I ever mention that you must be very specific when asking Mou a question? I attempted to be more specific by asking, "What is the range of their heights?"

Oh, anywhere from 8 to 15 feet. They are from a place with less gravity so they are tall. Small shape changers are 3 feet to 5 because they have more gravity.

"Are the Grays shapeshifters?"

No, but they influence light and density thus are invisible.

I guess that explains why we have never seen a fifteen-foot-tall gray alien. Next, I asked, "For those of you that can see them, would you describe them for me?"

Biped. Sense environment with 2 glands on a thin frame.

"What type of skin do they have?"

Many layers that protect them from almost anything.

"What is their average life span?"

Varies, adult in 200 years.

If it takes them 200 years to become an adult, they must be living around 700 of our years. I asked if they were multidimensional.

Yes, but must follow a trail.

I had no idea what he was talking about in following a trail. "What kind of a trail?" I asked.

Elemental and vibrational.

Once again, this was beyond my understanding. I tried to change the subject. "What is their relative intelligence compared with other advanced species?"

They are best at finding trails of elemental energy.

"Do they have any particular mission when they are here on Earth?"

Teaching you about energy.

Despite all the bad publicity about the grays, they have a positive influence on humans.

Pleiadian

Another well-known alien type is referred to as Pleiadian. Sometimes they are mistakenly referred to as Nordics and are believed to be humanoids. It is thought that this alien type is most human-like in form and has been interacting with our race for thousands of years. I started by asking Mou if Pleiadians really existed. He replied:

Yes.

From everything I've read and heard, I believed them to be friendly to humans. My next question was, "Do we have anything to fear from them?"

No.

In my research and previous conversations, I had only seen positive things about Pleiadians. When I inquired what their purpose was here on our planet, he responded.

To help with man's evolution.

"Have they been on our planet for a long period of time?"

Beyond your comprehension of time.

I guess I could translate that answer in two ways. They have been here for a really long time or I am too stupid to understand. It was time to change the subject so I asked, "Are they from the Milky Way?"

Yes.

"What is the life span of a Pleiadian?"

900 of your years.

When I asked Mou if he would describe one the answer was:

Same as you.

"Are you saying to me that they look just like humans?"

Yes.

"You are telling me that there is no way humans can tell they are communicating with a Pleiadian?"

No way.

I thought I would find out just how friendly they are with earthlings, so I asked if they breed with humans.

Yes.

That answer certainly opened a world of possibilities. Next, I inquired how long they've been breeding with humans. He replied:

A long time.

"Is there any way that a human can tell that they are having sex with a Pleiadian?"

No.

I guess he really meant there was no way you could tell a Pleiadian was different from a human. This answer could have brought up an entire new line of questioning, but I decided to ignore it for now. I asked if Pleiadians were ever born here on Earth.

Sometimes.

Connie and I have been told before that we both have alien DNA and that it dated back to our great-grandfathers. As I was asking the question, I had the strange feeling I already knew the answer. I asked what type of alien DNA we had in our blood.

Pleiadian.

"Are they residents of Earth?"

No.

"Do they live on other planets?"

Yes.

The next time you are walking down a crowded street, think about the fact that you might be interacting with extraterrestrials that look exactly like humans. The same logic might also apply the next time you think about having a one-night stand. Alien interaction may be much closer than you ever imagined.

Arcturians

I asked a guide what type of extraterrestrial being had the largest population on Earth. He replied:

Arcturians.

That being said, I thought it would be appropriate to spend some time discussing them. Famed psychic Edgar Cayce taught that beings from Arcturus are the most advanced culture in the Milky Way. That certainly covers a lot of real estate! He went on to say their planet was a prototype of the Earth's future. Arcturians act as spiritual healers in anticipation of the future of the human race. Much has been written by Norma Milanovich with Betty Rice and Cunthya Ploski in their book *We, the Arcturians,* in which they channel information from the Arcturians. One night we asked Mou if the information in their book was correct, and he answered:

Accurate in some ways.

One subject discussed in their book is that there will be a rebirth for humanity on Earth. "Are they accurate in their discussion about the rebirth?"

Yes.

"Can you tell us how this rebirth for humanity will actually take place?"

Life will be more important to life.

When I read their book, I got the idea they were the most advanced culture in our galaxy. When I asked Mou if that was true, the answer was:

No.

"Is there any culture in the Milky Way that is more advanced than others?"

No.

"Is their role to lead humanity into the future?"

No.

"What is the role of the Arcturians?"

To influence and to teach.

That could be interpreted to help lead us into the future. When I asked how they communicated with humans, the answer was:

Through thoughts and emotions.

The book also mentions that the Arcturians maintain a large craft that is dedicated to protecting the Earth. "Is that accurate?"

No.

"When Arcturians pass, do they go to the same Heaven as human souls?"

Yes, for sake of simplifying.

"When they reincarnate, do they come back as humans?"

Not so much as they have a human experience while on your planet.

"What is the average life span, in Earth years, of an Arcturian?"

800.

"Are they shapeshifters?"

They can shift.

I guess that explains why they do not have to reincarnate to have the human experience. They just shift shapes and blend in with the rest of us. "When Arcturians are on their own planet, what is their life expectancy in our years?"

Hundreds of your decades.

Once again it is apparent that humans get the short end of the stick when it comes to life spans. It seems like all advanced cultures live a lot longer than humans.

Little Whites

I always thought that much of the prehistoric cave paintings were Little Whites. As you will see in this next portion of the chapter, my perceptions of this alien type were quite mistaken. This alien type will also require a very open mind. I started by asking the height of a Little White.

3 feet.

At least that jived with my concepts of them. Next, I had Mou give me a physical description.

They are kind with a smooth skin-like exterior.

"What is their average life span?"

70.

That is quite short for an advanced species. When I asked if they had any special characteristics, Mou answered.

Healers.

"What is their mission on Earth?"

To teach healing.

"Who do they heal?"

Your humans.

"How do they heal humans?"

Raising their state of consciousness for self healing.

"Are you telling me that many of our natural healers are working with the aid of the Little Whites?"

Yes, without their understanding of such.

Many of the psychics and spiritual healers definitely have a unique ability to heal maladies in humans. Connie and I have taken a Reiki course in the past and have seen examples of the short-term healing effects. I asked him if the mental energies of the Little Whites assist in holistic practices such as Reiki. He replied:

Yes, many works of energy are being taught. Helping to open up your species is the hope.

I assumed that there were a lot of these guys present on Earth, assisting our healers. When I asked Mou if there were many of them here on our planet, I did not receive the answer I expected.

They do not work on Earth. They work from their own home.

"You are saying the Little Whites are not physically on Earth."

Yes, you project an image. Consciousness creates matter. You create your reality.

Needless to say, I was having a little trouble understanding how beings could work from a home that was thousands of light years away. I asked the name of the planet that was home to the Little Whites.

Bnuw.

Never heard of that one! I thought I would try to narrow down the location so I asked if it was in the Milky Way.

Yes.

"Can you describe their planet for me?"

Star.

I thought all the stars were like our sun and unbelievably hot. My next question was: "How can they be from a star?"

In your terms.

It is times like this that I realize just how uninformed this particular human can be. I tried to clarify that Little Whites actually came from a star. He answered:

Blue.

"A blue star?"

Yes, you asked.

"Is the blue star from a constellation we know?"

No.

I said to him, "Do you realize how this information is messing up my concepts of what takes place around us?"

You asked. That is a human thing.

I think there was a bit of disdain for humans in that comment. It was time to change the subject, so I asked if they had any specific type of space craft.

No.

"How do they travel?"

They transport mentally.

That answer opened up a new concept in transportation. I replied, "You mean they do not require vehicles to move around in the galaxy."

Yes.

"What is their communication method?"

Mind.

"Are they shapeshifters?"

No, through manipulation of thought.

The more I learn about the Little Whites, the more I am impressed. Everything they accomplish is by mind manipulation from a distance of many light years.

Nordics

Nordics get a lot of play on the Internet. They are portrayed as being tall and good-looking. When I asked how tall the height of a Nordic, the answer was:

7.

That would certainly make them stand out. Another characteristic of a Nordic is said to be blond hair. However, the answer when I inquired if they all had the same hair color was:

No.

"Do all of them look like humans?"

All are human.

I assume from that answer that Nordics have been around for so long that they are totally assimilated into the human form. The answer when I inquired into their mission was:

Guide others.

This seems to be why there is an alien presence here on Earth, to guide and help humans to evolve, in spite of ourselves.

Zetas

The Zetas are said to come from the star system, Zeta Reticuli and are best known for being supposedly responsible for the abductions of Betty and Barney Hill in the 1960s. Their abduction is quite interesting, and the details can be read at www.skepticreport.com. When I inquired if Betty and Barney were really abducted, the answer was:

Yes.

When I asked if they were from Zeta Reticuli, he answered:

No.

"Where do they come from?"

Saturn.

Once again I was not expecting that answer, but we were told there were light beings from that planet. I asked if they were light beings.

Yes.

"Are you saying that Zetas are light beings that are from the planet Saturn?"

Moon.

"Do you know which moon, after all there are sixty-five of them, both named and unnamed."

No.

Such an abrupt answer is one way to end a discussion. Some of the websites refer to them as the small grays. All of the previous answers were from another guide. When I asked Mou if the Zetas exist, he replied:

Yes, they are from another world, not like me.

I guess I should have asked him what the "not like me" meant. My next question inquired what the Zetas were.

Subculture. They are a cousin to the shapeshifters. They cannot change as much as the shape changers. They are limited to who they look like. They cannot cross with Earth. Too far apart in DNA. More like Grays.

At least we don't have to worry about a Zeta trying to seduce our women. "Are there many Zetas here on Earth?"

No.

"What is the purpose for the Zetas being here on this planet?"

A question.

That was not a very positive answer if another alien cannot figure out why they are here. I changed the subject by asking, "How tall is a Zeta?"

3 ft.

"What do they look like?"

Cute.

I think he was trying to duck the questions. What may be cute to a guide or another extraterrestrial may not be cute to us. In a later session I attempted to get more detail as to their appearance.

Somewhat like your reptiles.

That does not sound overly cute. When I asked the role of a Zeta, the guide replied:

All come with similar purposes.

Whenever I ask the question of what motivates advanced cultures to visit our planet, the answer is always positive. From the human point of view, that is a good thing. In my research, I ran across writings that referred to Zetas as light people. I asked the guide if they were indeed referred to as light people.

Man may call them whatever, yes.

"Are Zetas in regular communication with earthlings?"

Not so much.

I am not sure we know a lot more about Zetas than when we started.

Sirian Hybrid

I attempted to check on the Internet to get information about what is published about Sirian Hybrids. Each site had a different rendition of information about this alien type. While I have a pretty good imagination, some of what I read was really out there. I figured the only way to really find out anything on this alien type was to ask Mou. My first question was, "Is there such a thing as a Sirian Hybrid?"

Yes.

"What is a Sirian?"

An influence from Sirius.

"Is Sirius a planet?"

More star like.

"Where does it come from?"

Many lifetimes away.

I could tell he was not exactly giving me detailed answers. "Can you describe one?"

They are very old souls.

That was not the answer to my question. I tried another subject. "Are they still visitors to our planet?"

Oh, yes.

"What is their role?"

They watch over animals.

Sometimes it is just better to give up and move on.

Beings from Other Galaxies

At this point you have been hearing about beings that have come from our own galaxy, the Milky Way. While the distance between galaxies is beyond the imagination of humans, travel between galaxies apparently takes place every day in the life of the extraterrestrials. I asked if beings from other planets could travel between the galaxies. His answer caught me by surprise.

As are you.

He did mention before that I had reincarnated on other planets in prior life. My guess is I traveled the stars in a distant lifetime, but I could not remember doing it. Knowing there is a committee that controls what happens in our galaxy, I inquired if living alien beings needed to get permission to travel between the galaxies. He replied:

No.

One night Mou told us that he brought along a Lbyn and a Bmt to help in writing my books. Not recognizing either of the names, I asked if they were extraterrestrial types. He replied:

Your aids to write.

I can use all the help I can get, but his answer did not match my question. I tried again, "Are they aliens?"

Yes.

"Are they from a different planet than where you come from?"

Yes, they are from other galaxies. We are from the Milky Way. They are from places your scientists have not seen.

No question my alien buddy has friends in faraway places. This was the first time we had confirmation of alien life in other galaxies. I asked if he would describe what they would have looked like.

Right, they are dead. Ha, ha, ha. All dead look the same.

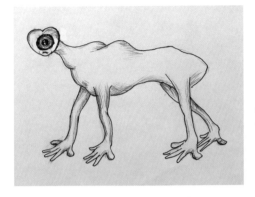

An extraterrestrial from another galaxy as described by Mou. *Sketch by Michael Longo.*

There goes that comedy thing again. I tried again, "Would you describe them for me when they were in body?"

When in bodies, they were on four legs with hands with three fingers and two thumbs. Their heads were round with one eye and a small mouth. They have small brains because they use most of it.

That description may seem a little strange to the average human, but as we found out, there are some out-of-the-ordinary beings in our own Milky Way.

Shapeshifters

My grandchildren used to watch a TV show in which there were shapeshifters. I remember making fun of them and telling them there could be no such being. Every once in a while, it becomes necessary to eat one's own words. I was to find out that the presence of shapeshifters is a very real phenomenon. My first real encounter with the shapeshifter reality was when I was questioning Mou about the alien abduction of Connie several years ago in Florida and how her car traversed over twenty miles of the Florida Turnpike without her being in the car. When I asked how they managed the event, he said:

It is easy when you know how. We put a shapeshifter in the car.

From that time on, I definitely have added respect for that alien type. With the possibility that we could have well-known people who were really aliens, one night I asked him if any of our famous humans really were shapeshifters. His answer shed a little light on the issue.

Some.

I could not resist trying to find out who they were. When I asked for names, he replied:

Burbfmrw.

Sometimes he gives me a garbage answer rather than a direct answer. This is usually for my personal protection. Connie jumped in and asked if this was his way of saying he was not going to answer.

Yes.

In one of my very first sessions with Mou I asked him if there were extraterrestrial beings that looked like humans. His answer was:

There are two that shape change. They can morph to look like you. All others need to hide.

So you can see that shapeshifters really do exist and there are multiple extraterrestrial types that can change their form.

Spider People

The Nazca Line spider in Peru. Dollar Photo Club.

What I consider one of the most interesting images in the Nazca Lines is the one in the shape of a spider. When I asked Mou what the shape of the spider stood for, he informed me that it was the shape of the aliens that were present at the time the lines were constructed. He also told me that they stood around six feet. Certainly not the place for anyone with Arachnophobia! In a later session I inquired if spider people were still present on Earth. Thankfully, he answered:

No.

"Did the Spider People used to be here on Earth?"

Yes.

"Do they still exist on other planets?"

Yes.

"How tall did they stand?"

6 feet.

I thought I would double check for my friends that are very fearful of spiders, so I restated the question by asking if they are just not here on Earth. He reiterated his former reply.

Yes.

I think I could just hear a large sigh of relief from many of you reading this chapter. I must admit, no matter how openminded an individual, it would be unnerving to look out my window and see a six-foot spider.

And Even Types You've Never Heard About

Sometimes when I ask Mou questions, I have absolutely no idea what he is talking about. When I asked if there were any additional alien beings that visited Earth, he replied:

Kcr's and Mocors.

Those names were not exactly part of my daily vocabulary. I inquired if humans were familiar with Kcr's and Mocors and he answered:

No.

"Are they shapeshifters?"

No

"Are they reptilian?"

No.

As you can see, I was not getting anywhere fast with my questions. I decided to ask how tall they were.

6 ft.

At least he answered one question. I made one more attempt: "Have they ever been seen by humans?"

No.

As you will see in other chapters, there are many more types of beings than I've described in this chapter. In fact, there are many more types than I've ever imagined. There are light beings from Saturn and green ones from Pluto, just to name a few more. The number of beings from other worlds is only limited by our imagination and our own ability to travel the stars and learn what is really out there.

CHAPTER 6

NATURE OF THE UNIVERSE, SPACE, AND WORMHOLES

Even with our new telescopes, we only have a rudimentary knowledge of space and our galaxy. Space is repeatedly referred to as the last frontier. Since the invention of the telescope 600 years ago, we have made so many significant advances. The more we learn, the more we find out how much more there is to learn. Humans can only understand emotions and understandings that they have experienced. You will soon realize how little we have actually experienced.

The whole concept of being able to rapidly travel through the vast expanses of space defies the imagination. Our methods of space travel must be exceedingly slow and rudimentary compared to the speeds needed to travel from the far reaches of our galaxy. For instance, an estimate of the time it would take to get to Mars using current technology is 260 days. In previous conversations with Mou, he said that their ships can travel at twice the speed of light. Even traveling at twice the speed of light, it would take a huge amount of time to transverse the immense distances in our universe. There has to be something about the method of travel for aliens that we do not know.

I was always told in school that space is a vacuum. One thing I realized while communicating with Mou is that what is very clear to his mind is not necessarily very clear to mine, even though I know he dumbs down the information so I have some chance to digest it. One of the most difficult concepts for me to comprehend is the beginning of the Universe.

Our Universe, Starting Out with a Bang!

How do you understand something so huge that it has no beginning and no end? Even more difficult is trying to understand how something that has no beginning or end was created. One of the theories that has gained a lot of popularity about the creation of our universe is the Big Bang hypothesis. What follows is an explanation of the theory that appears in www.universetoday.com.

The basics of the Big Bang theory are fairly simple. In short, the Big Bang hypothesis states that all of the current and past matter in the Universe came into existence at the same time, roughly 13.8 billion years ago. At this time, all matter was compacted into a very small ball with infinite density and intense heat called a Singularity. Suddenly, the Singularity began expanding, and the universe as we know it began.

Working backwards from the current state of the Universe, scientists have theorized that it must have originated at a single point of infinite density and finite time that began to expand. After the initial expansion, the theory maintains that the Universe cooled sufficiently to allow the formation of subatomic particles, and later simple atoms. Giant clouds of these primordial elements later coalesced through gravity to form stars and galaxies.

This all began roughly 13.8 billion years ago, and is thus considered to be the age of the universe. Through the testing of theoretical principles, experiments involving particle accelerators and high-energy states, and astronomical studies that have observed the deep universe, scientists have constructed a timeline of events that began with the Big Bang and has led to the current state of cosmic evolution.

That explanation pretty much sums up the current state of scientific theory concerning the formation of the Universe. I asked Mou if there was any truth behind the Big Bang theory. His reply was:

Yes, in part.

When I asked him if he could explain how the Universe was created, he once again deflated my ego by stating:

That is beyond your comprehension.

It is a good thing my feelings are not easily hurt. I asked a question that I figured I would be able to understand: "Is the Universe expanding or contracting?"

Expanding.

"Does the Universe have any limits?"

Not as such.

I find it very hard to comprehend something that has no limits getting larger. I asked, "So the Universe is actually getting bigger all the time?"

Yes.

I ran across a website that actually attempted to define the size of our galaxy, the Milky Way, and the Universe as a whole. According to www.bbc.com, our galaxy measures from 100,000 light years to 150,000 light years in width. They then went on to estimate the size of the Universe as 93 billion light years in diameter. In case you were wondering, light travels 186,000 miles per second. If you do the math, that equates to 5.87849981 x 10,000,000,000,000 or approximately, 5,878,499,810,000 miles in a year. In comparison, as I write this chapter, our National Debt is around $20,000,000,000,000. I just thought I would throw that in to give everyone something to think about. As a final question on this subject, I asked Mou, "How many galaxies are there?"

Billions of galaxies. We have not cracked but maybe 5%. Think of the possibilities.

I read that the current assumption is that all suns have planets, and there are millions of suns in a galaxy. If you follow that logic through to a conclusion, there are trillions of planets out there—an unfathomable number of opportunities for intelligent life. It is absolutely astounding to me how people can doubt there is intelligent life on one of these trillions of planets, but many do.

Nature of Space

I always thought that space was this huge area of nothingness. A vacuum where nothing could exist. One evening Mou made a statement that changed the way I thought about the vast emptiness that surround our planets.

Ok. The space that looks empty to you is really filled with a fluid like, yet solid, substance.

That is definitely a statement that you will not find in the science books. I asked him for clarification.

Space is like water. It moves and it calms. While it is calm nothing happens. It looks pretty and nothing can get done. So like the wind something moves and starts the storm. The more it moves, the more can get done. We can move around the Universe. Then it calms and we get stuck.

The idea that space moves like a sea that has tides was a new concept. One evening with another guide, I attempted to verify the concept that space was like the water in the ocean. I asked if space really does ebb and flow. He answered:

Yes.

"Is it calm around Earth?"

Low Tide.

I will take that answer to mean that we are in a relative calm part of space. My next question was, "If space is really a liquid, what is the composition of the liquid?"

Carbon, Nitrogen.

Assuming the information is correct, we have an awful lot to learn. I changed the subject and asked, "Are there any areas of space where it is safe to travel?"

Safe is relative.

"What makes areas of space more dangerous?"

Uninhabitable.

We were again heading down the road of circular logic, and the odds of me getting an answer that I could understand were diminishing. I replied, "What makes it uninhabitable?"

That which is required to live.

Sometimes when I am communicating with Mou I get the idea that he had to be a lawyer in a past life. Trying to get a straight answer can be like pulling teeth. I tried another approach and asked if oxygen was required for life. He answered:

Perhaps.

I don't think I gained a whole lot of knowledge from that exchange. He told me in the past that on his planet they breathed a nitrogen-rich atmosphere. I followed up by asking, "What is a characteristic of the thousands of planets that have intelligent life?"

All need a fluid like water and a temperature moderate. The planet must have gravity and it must circulate, like have wind and tides. Have a good atmosphere to hold life.

He mentioned wind and tides. Since our moon is responsible for the tides, I asked him the purpose of a moon. He replied:

To make life. Without the moon, Earth is lifeless. It is the Earth's lungs.

Now that we are totally mixed up about the nature of space, let's switch the subject to something we have all heard about: wormholes. If you are like me, you have no real knowledge of them other than the cool name and that they get talked about a lot.

Wormholes

The theory of wormholes originated in 1935, when Albert Einstein and Nathen Rosen proposed the existence of paths or bridges through time and space. Based on the theory of general relativity, these bridges would connect two different locations in space and time creating a shortcut that would reduce the time/space distance. I would be lying if I told you I understood what I just typed. I did ask Mou if the aliens gave Einstein his ideas about wormholes. His answer did not surprise me.

They did.

Once again it appears we have to thank our visitors from outer space for assisting our great human thinkers. Wormholes have been a very popular subject on television for the past couple of years. If you listen to Morgan Freeman, the moderator of the show based on them (*Through the Wormhole*), it is quite entertaining, but everything is based on conjecture and theoretical assumptions about a subject that we really know nothing about. Space.com defines wormholes as: "A theoretical passage through space-time that could create shortcuts for long journeys across the universe." Einstein also warned of the danger that a wormhole could rapidly collapse. In order to simplify the whole issue of wormholes, I asked my alien guide what a wormhole really was.

It is like a tunnel, and you can get in one of these things and time speeds up. You can move faster than light. Because time rules speed, there are no limits. You go from one place to the next with ease, but they can collapse on you.

So Einstein was correct when he mentioned that a wormhole could collapse. I am not sure that answer really simplified my understanding of wormholes. After considering the answer for several weeks I made up some additional questions about the subject. I asked him if he could describe a wormhole.

Artist concept of a wormhole. Dollar Photo Club.

EZ. You know one of those china handheld fans. The ones that fold out to show a picture. While it is folded, you drill a hole from one wooden handle to the next. The distance between the two handles is about an inch. It is a short distance. Now open the fan all the way open. It is a long distance. The space moves like this fan, opening and closing. Like the sea has tides. It moves and breathes and rips and you can shoot through it. Well, if you see a place that is folded up like the closed fan and you shoot a hole through it, you can go from one side of the fan to the other in only an inch travel, but when the fan opens you have a route to travel. So space is this fan opening and closing. EZ.

I really hate it when he starts or ends an explanation with EZ. I know from experience that what is easy for Mou is not exactly easy for me. At least I could relate to the Chinese fan example.

Like a Rock in a Pond

Simulation of a wormhole, a rock in a pond. Adobe Stock.

My next inquiry related to how a wormhole forms.

Like the stone in the pond.

I wasn't quite sure what he meant by that comment, but I found a pretty cool picture of a stone hitting the water and forming what looks like a small tunnel. When I asked him who throws the stone he gave me a one-word answer.

God.

Pretty hard to argue with that answer! I will assume he meant natural forces. He had mentioned earlier that sometimes a wormhole collapses. I did not see how being inside a wormhole that collapsed could have a happy ending. My thoughts were confirmed by his answer.

We have a funeral. There is some warning but it does happen. You get stretched into nothing.

At least there is some warning. It seems as though traveling through a wormhole is not without its risks. It might have seemed like an obvious question to my alien friend but my next question inquired if space craft traveled through wormholes.

Of course you do. It is primitive but still faster and simpler.

I guess I should have known that. The Universe is a pretty big place. If wormholes come and go, I was wondering how they knew where they went and where the exits were located.

You can see them. It takes the first trip through it to see where it goes. Then once you know where it goes you can drill other exits to get to other places, like a freeway. You have a road that goes from A to Z, and then along the way you begin wanting to see things so you cut next to all the side sights, but each time you cut one, you shorten its life.

The thought of seeing an exit when you were traveling at the speed of light seems to be right out of *Star Wars*. I often miss exits traveling at sixty mph. This whole wormhole thing was really getting complicated. In my mind it would take an awful lot of nerve to get into one just to see where it goes. What if you did not want to go there? I must admit that the idea of freeways in space is kind of cool. I asked him what it was like to be traveling in a wormhole. His answer described something I could relate to.

What it feels like driving in a snowstorm. Just about like that only there are colors.

As I write this I am considering what it would be like to travel through a snowstorm at the speed of light. I think it takes a lot of nerve to travel on alien ships. He had told us before that you just had to go faster than the speed of light to reverse time. I asked him if you could use wormholes to go back in time.

Not practical. You just go faster than time and in that you start to reverse. See, faster than light it is the speed of time. This is why time stands still when you reach the speed of light. A little faster than light is time and faster than time it reverses. EZ. It is in the math equation.

He used that EZ statement again. I guess it is relatively simple if you just think that the speed of light is the speed of time. To go back in time you just have to go faster than the speed of light. As Shakespeare said, "Aye, there's the rub." We are nowhere near approaching the speed of light.

From our conversations, I was getting the idea that there were quite a few wormholes around us. While writing this chapter, I was working at my home in Utah, so I asked if there were any of them currently near us. His answer was quite specific.

Three or four.

I was having trouble comprehending if there were wormholes near us, why we could not see them. I asked if when a wormhole forms a human could see it. His answer amplified how far humans still have to advance.

Not yet. Just because they do not know what to look for.

I figured this was my opening to get the information on trying to see a wormhole. I asked if he would tell me what to look for.

No.

That short and sweet answer shattered my hopes of gaining a piece of strategic knowledge. Since humans obviously have a long way to go, I inquired if all spirits are aware of wormholes.

No, only those advanced enough to look out.

I feel that I have only scratched the surface in my quest to learn a lot of information about wormholes. My assumption is that humans are not as yet ready to attempt utilizing wormholes as a mode of transportation. A civilization that cannot drive through snowstorms on Earth is certainly not ready to move through tunnels in space at the speed of light. If you don't believe me, just try driving around Washington, DC, after one inch of snow.

An Energy Vortex

We had discussed the use of an energy vortex at an earlier session. I asked him to compare traveling in wormholes with traveling on an energy vortex.

This is the best way but not the only way. My favorite way is like an energy to ride. It gets me places faster.

He just told us that you go faster than the speed of light in a wormhole, but you can ride an energy that is faster. This was starting to stretch even my imagination. I asked him to clarify what he was referring to.

They are a vortex. Each only come close to where you want to go. And you jump in and out of them where you want to go. It is faster than light. It is time reversing. You will have to talk to someone smarter than me to explain the math. Your energy to return and go happens all over the space continuum.

I asked him to tell me more about these energy vortexes.

There are vortexes that naturally happen that people run into that will take them from one place to the next. Some are time travel vortexes and move you from now to the past or future on Earth. There are vortexes that take you from Earth to other dimensions or planets. This is natural. It is Mother Nature that rules it and makes things in it. Since there is no time you do not age.

I especially like the part about where you do not age. My guess is that aliens can make a choice how you want to travel, much like we choose taking a train or bus. I asked him which mode of travel he preferred.

Vortexes are more stable, and if one ends, you just wait to jump another.

I think his description of jumping a vortex is a bit of an oversimplification. I inquired how you use a vortex to travel back in time. His answer once again seemed a bit of an oversimplification.

You just step into it.

At least he did not say easy. When I asked him if he had ever traveled back from the future he replied:

No, that is bad. It messes things up and it is bad on bodies. We can but we do not.

The whole thing about traveling faster than the speed of light seems to have the possibility of messing up your body. Since I was having the discussion with a deceased soul, I asked him if this mode of transportation was only for the souls of the departed. He answered:

I cannot think of any that are not. It never crossed my mind.

At least I came up with a question that made him think. I often get the impression that my questions are a bit boring for him.

Avoid the Squiggle!

I inquired if humans can see a vortex.

If you know what you are looking at.

You can probably anticipate my next question. It was "What do you look for?"

It looks like a squiggle. A bump in the picture. A flaw in the air.

Now we were getting somewhere! He actually gave me some information I could use. I asked if humans ever get into a vortex.

They do, back or forward.

I thought that could only happen in the movies. When I asked if it happened to many humans he replied:

Not a lot. It is a ripple in time.

I think the moral of this segment is quite clear. If you see a squiggle in the air, avoid it at all costs. You could find yourself re-fighting the Civil War.

Beyond Our Comprehension, Poof to Poof

The more I attempt to understand travel through space, the guides introduce concepts that are more and more difficult to comprehend. Humans conceive of travel as a vehicle being driven through space at relatively slow speeds. Using current technologies, it would take years or possibly even human lifetimes to reach places within our own solar system. If our galaxy is more than 100,000 light years in width, if the vehicle was capable of traveling twice the speed of light, it would take 50,000 years to cross the Milky Way. There has to be something about travel in space that humans are far from understanding. During a channeling session, I asked if there was any method of space travel other than wormholes or energy vortexes. He replied:

Yet to be discovered.

I knew there had to be a lot we did not understand, and it seems we are very far from discovering the true secrets to space travel. I posed the question, "If the galaxy is 100,000 light years across, how can ships travel such distances?"

Only you use the measure of time. Not traversed as you would.

He was once again eluding to the fact that we had no idea as to the technique used to transverse the expanses of space. When I asked the question, my psychic friend, Donna, and I were on the channeling board. She has the ability to mentally read some of the guides as they attempt to elaborate on more difficult questions. At this point of the session, she interjected that she was seeing that molecules have the ability to just transport from one place to another. This was a very difficult subject, and the guide was having a hard time describing the process. It was like an object was in one place, and *poof* it was in another place. She referred to it as *poof to poof,* and the object traversed a huge distance. I asked the guide if what Donna was describing was true. He replied:

Basically speaking.

"Are you saying the vast distances are covered by a process like molecular teleportation?"

Yes.

I think they put the term "molecular teleportation" into my head. I doubt I could have come up with it on the spur of the moment. My understanding of this system of transportation is like the concept of "beam me up, Scotty" from the old *Star Trek* series on television. Apparently the writers of the show knew a lot more about space travel then they admitted. As I discussed earlier, there has to be some method of transportation, far more advanced than anything conceived of by humans. This type of travel would seem to answer the question. Once again our guides had attempted to put us on a path to understanding a subject that seems to not be understandable. I thanked him for attempting to answer our questions. His reply seemed to be that of a parent speaking to a small child.

We are aware of all, try to assist.

It is impossible for us to comprehend the incredible technologies that are employed by the advanced cultures of the various galaxies. For the first time, we learned how it is possible to travel the vast expanses of space in a relatively short period of time: wormholes, energy vortexes, or molecular teleportation. Einstein discussed some of the phenomenon decades ago. It is only a matter of time until the visitors from outer space decide to feed us more of the information needed to travel the stars. Until that time we will just have to be content with our sixty-five miles per hour speed limits.

CHAPTER 7

SPACE TRAVEL VEHICLES

The websites of ufologists around the world are inundated by images of flying objects that are attributed to visitors from outside our planet. Unfortunately, most of the images would better be attributed to Photoshop. Movies from *Star Wars* to *2001 A Space Odyssey*, have images of flying ships that range from flying behemoths to small craft that zip rapidly from place to place. If we have indeed been visited by aliens since the time of the dinosaurs, they must have some incredible craft to traverse the galaxies at speeds much faster than light. In this chapter we will investigate the various types, sizes, and characteristics of the crafts used by our extraterrestrial visitors.

I started out by asking Mou how many types of space craft exist. His answer gave a lot of opportunity for investigation.

All in all, hundreds. Some so small as a baseball.

Assuming what he just said is accurate, that is a lot of different types of vehicles. In the movies, we always see the spaceships shooting at each other or even humans with various types of weapons. With their advanced technologies, I could only guess at the power of their weapons. When I inquired if the vehicles carried weapons, he answered:

No.

That is proof that cultures really can survive peacefully. Our military certainly carries all types of weapons on our aircraft and there are rumors on the Internet of our planes becoming involved in dogfights with aliens. My next question was, "Can alien craft be shot down by humans?"

No.

Once again, the movies do not get it close to correct. However, with hundreds of space vehicles to choose from, it is quite possible that some of the photographs on the Internet are accurate after all. Not only does it take a lot of vehicle types, the distances traveled are so huge that there must certainly be a technology far beyond our comprehension.

A Real Alien Drone

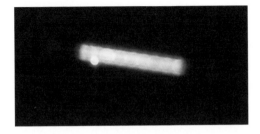

Photograph of an alien drone. Barry Strohm.

Another view of the alien drone. Barry Strohm.

If you read my previous book, you saw that I had a personal encounter with a small alien vehicle that resembled a bar of light. It happened on the Gettysburg battlefield while I was taking photographs for my first book. The object followed me for probably ten minutes, and I took more than forty frames of it on three different cameras. When I asked Mou to verify that the image I photographed that night in Gettysburg while ghost hunting was really an alien vehicle, he replied:

Yes.

When I asked him the purpose of the small vehicle, I think his answer avoided the question.

They were ghost hunting too.

Did I mention before that he has a great sense of humor? He also ducked my question quite nicely, but he did later confirm that it was a type of extraterrestrial drone. All I know is that it is a little eerie to realize that something is following you, and you are by yourself in the dark on one of the most haunted battlefields in the world. One interesting fact about my interaction with the drone is that I could not see the object with my eyes while I was photographing it. I was aware of the drone's presence by observing the screens on the back of my cameras.

When I started asking questions concerning the size of extraterrestrial vehicles it became very apparent how little we really understand about how our neighbors get around out there. When watching movies like *Star Wars* or various television shows, you hear names like "mothership," "supply ship," or maybe even a "death star." The answers from Mou were in many cases stranger than the fiction of the movies.

The Supply Ship

At the time we started learning about space craft, I thought the mothership was the largest of all the vessels. At least that is what I heard on television. When I asked Mou if a mothership could carry a supply ship, he said:

> A mothership cannot carry a supply ship. A supply ship can hold three motherships.

"What is the size of a supply ship?"

> Twice the size of a carrier.

That is getting very close to a half-mile in size. That must be one heck of a big vehicle! When I asked him the size of a supply ship, he really caught my attention.

> 2,300 feet.

At the time he told us this I did not realize a supply ship was relatively small in the whole spaceship size picture. I asked how fast a supply ship can go. He answered:

> Twice the speed of light.

That is really moving, especially for a vehicle almost 2,300 feet in size! My next question was, "What type of power do you use to propel a ship of that size?"

> A hybrid nuclear power.

There are obviously many sources of energy to power a space vehicle. So, the supply ship is the one that shuttles the motherships back and forth from the huge base vessel that we are told is hiding behind Saturn.

The Mothership

Anyone familiar with space jargon knows the term "mothership." I for one always thought that the proverbial mothership was the largest of the space vessels. As you now know, my guess was not even close. I started out by asking him the approximate size of a mothership. He answered:

> One Carrier.

For your information, the length of a *Nimitz* class carrier, the workhorse of our Navy, measures approximately 1,100 feet. Our carriers float on water with a maximum speed of fifty mph, while this alien craft flies through space at speeds faster than the speed of light. One evening I asked him the number of small craft the mothership holds. He replied:

Oh gee, 60, they are stored on three levels.

I could not resist the idea of finding out just how big their craft really were.

Big. OK. So a mothership is used like a carrier. It is where we can store other smaller ships.

Our carriers are manned by around 5,700 individuals, including the air wing. When I asked how many aliens are aboard a mothership he stated:

The mothership holds around 300. Each small ship holds from 4 to 9.

No question that extraterrestrial aircraft are manned in a more efficient manner than our large vessels. Most of the sightings by humans seem to be of smaller ships. I questioned him on what kind of a crew it takes to fly a small craft. As it turned out, their crews have a resemblance to our bomber crews.

Four. Pilot, sub-pilot, navigator, and engineer.

When I mentioned that the crew size sounded a lot like ours, he added more details.

Except for the engineer. Engineer plays with our motors more.

No matter how advanced the aircraft becomes, it appears it still takes a personal touch to keep the motors running. This also appears to be the size of vehicle that is plagued with mechanical problems and crashes.

A Ship the Size of Idaho

If you think some of their ships are almost unimaginable in size, NASA slipped up and, in 2015, published a photograph of the sun that included what appears to be an extraterrestrial craft the size of the state of Idaho. When I asked Mou what appeared in the image he replied:

A ship.

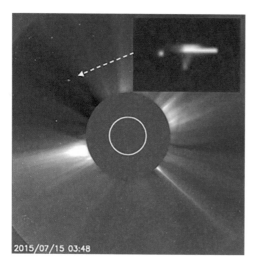

2015/07/15 03:48

Huge alien craft photographed near sun. NASA.

I was blown away by the thought that one of their vessels would actually be that large; after all, Idaho is a pretty big state. When I asked if it was really that big. He said:

Yes.

I asked him how it is possible that the vehicle could stand the extreme temperatures encountered by being that close to the sun. His reply was:

They are advanced.

Sometimes his answers are a bit understated. My next question inquired as to the purpose of the huge vessel.

Study.

"Are they studying Earth?"

Yes.

"Is it controlled by the galactic committee?"

Yes.

That was a relief. The thought of a ship the size of Idaho in unfriendly hands would be quite unnerving. There are rumors of Earth cooperating in deep-space experiments, so I asked if our government was involved with the mission of the huge ship.

No.

And I thought that everything I read on the Internet was true! I imagined this would have to be the mother of all motherships. When I asked if it was some type of a home base for visitations to Earth, the answer was:

Some.

When I asked my alien spirit friend if there were any ships larger than this one, the reply was:

Yes.

I was really expecting him to answer in the negative. I replied with, "What is the size of the largest ship in the extraterrestrial fleet?"

I do not know what you call it.

What is the purpose of the largest ship?

Allows us to live among you.

If you have any doubts about an alien presence on Earth, that answer should help alleviate any remaining doubts.

You Thought a Ship the Size of Idaho Was Big?

I repeated the question. "How large is the largest ship?"

Size compares to your United States.

I was not expecting that answer. It is very hard to imagine a vehicle that is 3,000 miles from one edge to the other! Mou has been known to pull my leg, so I asked him if there really was a huge ship the size of the US. He reiterated his previous answer.

Yes.

Next, I asked where this huge ship was currently located. He replied:

Mobile, there are many who visit.

That answer gives you an idea of just how many extraterrestrial beings are visiting Earth at any one time. Next, I asked if any of the visitors are from other galaxies.

Some.

It is becoming more obvious that vast distances seem to be no obstacle to Earth visitations. "Are any of these huge ships near Earth now?"

Only 1.

"Are there space stations where the other vehicles come to restock?"

This is it.

By current standards, I can only imagine how much fuel a vehicle of that size requires. I asked, "Does this vehicle ever have to refuel?

No.

This is definitely a concept unheard of to humans. We had discussed a currently-unheard-of method of transportation in earlier sessions that I described in an earlier chapter. My next question suggested that the huge vehicle traveled using this method. "Does a vehicle this size also move by molecular teleportation?"

Yes.

That would explain how they can travel such long distances in a relatively short period of time, but I still find this whole process unimaginable. I would guess that a base ship of this size would have a huge crew on board. I asked if different types of aliens would be aboard this vehicle. He replied:

Yes.

How many different types of extraterrestrial beings would be aboard a ship of this size?"

250.

I did not even know there *were* 250 different types of aliens! I had to make sure I got the message correctly, so I rephrased it. "You are saying that there are 250 different types of beings on that one single vehicle?"

Yes.

And I thought my chapter on alien types was fairly complete. I have a hard time believing that something flying around the size of the United States cannot be seen through our telescopes, so I asked the question, "Why can we not see the ship through our large telescopes?"

It is behind Saturn.

"So it is hiding behind Saturn?"

Yes.

"Can this huge ship travel faster than the speed of light?"

Yes.

It is truly hard to comprehend that a flying vehicle can actually be larger than the United States and move by molecular teleportation. It certainly adds a new dimension to the "beam me up, Scotty" concept I was used to. In previous chapters you learned that Mou is from the planet Robbe. I asked him how far it was from Robbe to Earth. He replied:

345 light years.

"If you travel by molecular teleportation, how long would it take to get from your planet to Earth?"

Two days.

I have no idea how to translate that into mph but it is certainly an indication of how much we have to learn.

Resupplying a Spaceship

As we are all aware, any travel here on Earth requires a continuous process of refueling our automobiles. It seems to me that traveling around the Milky Way at speeds faster than the speed of light would require a vast network of fuel and restocking facilities. My first question on this subject was, "Do space vehicles have to refuel?"

No.

That was not the answer I was expecting! My follow-up question was, "Are there any restocking bases in our solar system?"

No, there is no need to restock.

Why not?

They do not have the same requirements. Needs, simply put.

I don't think his words, "simply put" were a compliment. What he is telling us is that whatever fuel they use in their vehicles, it is self-sustaining. I asked, "How is it possible that space vehicles do not need a place to refuel on Earth?"

Fuel is of lower dimension.

I think that is a nice way of saying it was time to change the subject.

Avoiding Detection

In multiple sessions, I attempted to find out why a ship the size of United States can operate without being observed. The first time I asked the question, he replied:

Advanced equipment.

Sometimes he really simplifies answers for me. When I rephrased the question and asked why the motherships could not be seen, his answer made a lot more sense.

We just go stealth. We have shown your scientists the simple forms of this. We change an electron force so light goes through us. We are there, you just cannot detect us.

I guess that makes sense if you say it real fast. To an alien it is not a big deal to alter an electron force. Think about how advanced a civilization would have to be to make a craft as large as four football fields disappear. It seems as though humans have an incredible amount to learn if we are to take our place among the advanced cultures. I always kind of thought they might alter their mass or something. My next inquiry was, "Are you saying you don't change size or shape?"

Right, we cannot change our mass, just hide it. Mass is hard to change. It can be done, but it takes too much energy. We cannot hold that much energy in a ship, so we play with the way we look.

So they really can change mass. It is just that it takes a lot of energy. There seems to be no end to what the extraterrestrials can accomplish.

Travel in Other Dimensions

The concept of other dimensions is a very difficult one to understand. In fact, sometimes I have no clue what he is talking about. One evening I asked him what can be found in the other dimensions. He replied:

Other places of life. Other people and new unmanned planets.

I know that it is possible for creatures such as Bigfoot to be multidimensional too and use that ability to avoid detection. When I asked if extraterrestrials had the ability to make their vehicles multidimensional, his reply was:

Yes.

Is that one of the reasons that we cannot see them?

Yes.

They have many methods of remaining unseen while visiting on Earth. When I asked the guide how many dimensions there were, he answered:

7.

When I asked him if he would describe these other dimensions, he replied:

No.

I guess we will have to save the subject of other dimensions for another book when the guides are in a more informative humor.

The Fleet

The way Mou explains it, there is the equivalent of a task force that moves around in space that consists of many different vehicles. The main vehicle is approximately the size of the United States. As I wrote this chapter, it was apparently hiding from view behind Saturn. This ship acts as a base camp and holds several supply ships. A supply ship is capable of holding three motherships. A mothership is the approximate size of one of our aircraft carriers and holds a crew of around 300 individuals. The mothership holds around sixty small vehicles that are stored on three levels. Each of these small ships have a crew of four or five individuals. In addition, they have access to hundreds of smaller vehicles or drones to use as they observe the human evolution. Keep in mind that all this activity is going on around us and we have no clue.

Landing Sites, Then and Now

In earlier conversations, he had inferred that it took huge areas of solid rock to hold the really large ships. The Palpa Flat Mountain in Peru is an example of an area that was excavated for such a landing spot. I asked him to explain why such a large landing area was required for their aircraft.

The ships are so big and heavy in Earths' gravity that when they land on Earth they sink. For this reason they need a solid place to land on and turn the ship off. The mountain of rock will hold them. They can come to supply their needs without landing, but it takes a lot of fuel. So to make it easier, we make a landing place to hold the ship solid.

Alien landing site in Peru, the Palpa Flat Mountain. *Dreamstime.*

To get an idea of the massive area required for a landing site, I have included a picture of the Palpa Flat Mountain located near the Nazca Lines in Peru. Keep in mind that this landing area was constructed well over 1,000 years ago.

Mou told us their supply ships are larger than four football fields. No wonder they need such large landing areas. It is almost inconceivable that a flying craft that large cannot be detected visually or by our radar systems.

If we have the huge space vehicles in near proximity of our Earth, how do they interact with humans? One question I have is how all that activity keeps from colliding with our satellites. Mou answered with a quite simple answer.

Beyond your satellites.

How do your ships keep from getting hit by space junk or meteorites?

We are advanced.

At this stage of our book, I do not think he needs to reiterate how advanced our neighbors from outer space really are. In ancient times there were landing areas for large ships, especially in Peru. I asked, "Are there any landing sites for extraterrestrial vehicles on Earth?"

Not for the large ships, only smaller craft.

"Where are the current landing sites on Earth?"

They do not remain the same.

"Are there underground landing sites?"

More than above.

I could see he was starting to get evasive. "Are there a lot of underground landing sites?

Not so much.

There are times when he is not going to give definitive information on a subject. This was one of those times. I tried asking, "Are the sites for the smaller crafts under water?"

No, underground.

"Does our government know there are landing sites?"

Some. We are in agreement.

"Is there a landing site in the Antarctic?"

Yes.

When I asked more questions about Antarctica I realized that this topic deserved a chapter of its own, and you will find it as the final chapter in this book. Next, I inquired, "How about Iraq?"

Yes.

I could see we were not going to learn detailed information on the number or location of alien bases, just enough detail to keep our interest. One thing is obvious: There are more sites than we imagined. In addition, our government is doing a great job of keeping their side of the treaty.

Sharing Alien Technologies

After hearing the incredible size and capabilities of the extraterrestrial space vehicles, it seems like an impossible task for the human race to catch up with beings from other planets. He has told us in the past about how they have helped us advance through the ages. I asked Mou if different cultures share information with earthlings. He replied:

We have, to yours. We are an odd people. We want to prove God, too. Not all beings have the need to understand the difference between the now and the hereafter. We as a people have a need to know of what is after now. It is our karma, so we, like you, search for answers.

I am not sure if there is a reason that we have to rapidly learn the technology, but it would be nice if they accelerated our learning program. I asked Mou why they did not share more information with humans. He replied:

Ha ha ha. We have but you have egos and you cannot say look here, see what the blues gave us. We gave you the tiny cameras. Yes, you are welcome. You think you discovered radio waves, so see we do share.

The space beings apparently give us a lot more information than we give them credit for. I began to wonder if other cultures share information with each other. On Earth, each country does not want another to spy upon its technology. When I asked if extraterrestrial cultures shared information with each other, his answer was:

There is an openness, but we too have egos and want to be the first, the best, the fastest, and the best. So when it becomes every day, then we share, but we have egos too.

Like humans, the blues declassify and share technology after it becomes common knowledge. My guess is that if they gave us too much information, we would just use it to wage our wars more aggressively.

CHAPTER 8

THE GALACTIC COMMITTEE AND THE TREATY

Have you ever wondered why all the advanced cultures in our galaxy, with their incredible technology and weapons, have not destroyed or captured the less advanced planets, such as Earth? The answer is that they have learned the futility of mass destruction and that young or developing planets need to be protected and allowed to evolve. Once they have evolved, they can contribute to the universal community. Mou told us that, in past times, there was violence and arguments among the advanced members of our galaxy, but they learned that the violence only led to mutual destruction. When I asked him how they stopped it, he replied:

Committee was formed. Now there is not much disagreements.

In order to enforce mutual safety, a committee was formed among the advanced cultures that regulates the actions of all its members, kind of like a United Nations on an intergalactic scale. As an earthling, I find it very hard to believe that such a huge collection of advanced cultures could actually get along. Of course, the only thing I can compare it with is how our governments function here on Earth. I asked: "Is there ever conflict between galaxies?"

Not likely.

One evening during a channeling session, I asked Mou how long ago the committee was formed. He answered:

Our measure of time does not compare.

That was a fancy answer informing me that he was not going to answer. At a later session I thought I would try again and asked him how many years ago the commission was formed and his answer was:

177,312 years ago.

I am not sure if he was messing with me or not, but I think he was still ducking the question. In any event, our galaxy has been governed for a very long time. When I inquired if the commission was just for our galaxy, he said:

No.

This was the first time I'd heard about cooperation between galaxies. Since our culture is quite young, I inquired how long Earth was represented on the committee.

400 years.

That would be around the early 1600s, a time when humans were making rapid advancement in learning. "Are there any countries on Earth that are favored over others by the committee?"

No.

Next, I inquired, "How are extraterrestrial cultures selected to serve on the Committee?"

Fair representation.

"Is any Earth country represented?"

All. One planet, not separation.

I think he said that there is actually a venue where all the countries are fairly represented.

The more we learn, the more apparent it becomes that conflict is pretty much limited to the younger cultures, like Earth.

Functions of the Committee

According to Mou, the Committee has total governing power over the galaxy and beyond. Included in their responsibilities is protection of undeveloped planets, like ours. Extraterrestrials are require to get permission to come here and observe the local inhabitants.

All have to go thru the inter-planet committee to visit. We are not free to interfere. Advanced places are governed by a committee. We have to get ok to play on the planets with life.

My guess is they would like to come here to observe our thirst for bizarre behavior. I asked him what the aliens thought of our violence and wars.

You are a young people and you have much to settle and learn. As young planets go, you are rather peaceful. Other planets are more hostile, but some are peaceful. Now that I am without form I have studied many Gods and understand.

Apparently after you have passed and do not have a human form, your soul can learn more rapidly. With everything going on in the news, I felt compelled to ask, "Are humans considered a lower form of life?"

No, just young.

Visitors from other planets are supposed to play by the rules set up by the Committee. I asked him how the ruling body knows if one of the visitors is breaking the rules and influencing human development.

We have devices like cameras. They must carry at all times. So an alarm goes off if someone breaks a rule. If you choose to visit a planet you agree to follow protocol. This device monitors your feelings.

Amazingly, the Committee knows if you are planning to break a visitation rule! There is much we do not understand going on around us, including a very elaborate system protecting us from advanced cultures. My next question addressed what happens if an alien actually breaks a rule of the Committee.

They are punished by sanctions and expelled until they pay back the Committee with gifts for all the planets. A costly mistake. Yours is not the only planet we have restrictions on. There are thousands.

It is nice to know we are being protected. When I inquired as to the current state of relations between our planet and the commission, his message was quite positive.

There is peace among them.

As I write this chapter, it is the fall of 2016, and we are two weeks from our election for President. It has been one of the most contentious and nasty elections ever. I inquired if our relations with the committee would improve after the election. He answered:

The election has no bearing.

After the election it was determined that Donald Trump was the winner, and I asked another guide what they thought of the election results on the other side. We received a similar answer.

That is not of our world. Your reality is different from ours. We leave that up to you.

I guess in the really big picture, who gets elected to a political position in one country of our planet will really have no lasting effect on our long-term evolution.

Details about the Committee

When humans think of a committee, we think of a group of individuals getting together to discuss a matter or make a recommendation. The more I thought about it, the more it dawned on me that there would have to be an incredibly large group of individuals attempting to meet in one place. When I asked Mou if they met in one place, he answered:

No.

When I inquired, "How many members are on the committee?" there was no answer. The more information learned about the committee, the more I realized it must be huge in size to represent that many individuals. I tried again to get the information from another guide at a later time. This time he gave me a number.

5780.

I had a funny feeling about the answer so I asked him if it was accurate. He replied:

No.

Then I asked him if he really knew the number and he answered:

No.

My guess is that the size is the committee is a well-kept secret. Maybe they use email to keep in touch.

My next question inquired how often our government communicates with the committee that enforces the treaty. He replied:

Regularly.

The fact that our government has been following the guidelines of an intergalactic committee for many years indicates that our government can keep a secret. Next, I asked, "Who does the communicating with the committee.

Three people, not known publicly.

When I asked if other governments communicate with the committee on a regular basis the answer was:

Yes.

I asked if any governments are favored by the committee, and Mou replied:

We talk to those that can influence global events.

In multiple sessions, we discussed with Mou the agreement that existed between the countries on Earth and the committee. We will refer to this agreement or understanding as "the treaty." You will learn that this agreement has existed for many years.

Have you ever wondered the real reason that countries go to such extremes to prevent disclosure of the extraterrestrial presence on Earth? Through the years, people have been ridiculed, careers ruined, and persons committing suicide, all to prevent knowledge of alien events from being discovered. Any pilot in the military knows that reporting a UFO means the end of their career. Not only is the secret kept worldwide, there are serious penalties for anyone interested in public disclosure. The reason is that an agreement exists that dictates that the alien presence must remain undisclosed.

Countries of the world that would like to blow each other up seem to cooperate on at least one subject; keeping the secret of the alien presence. For any such non-disclosure agreement to be agreed upon by the countries on our planet, there would appear to be some kind of an understanding, or maybe even a treaty. Another possibility is that the fear of extraterrestrial retribution is so great that no other incentive is needed.

An Agreement for Peace and Cooperation

We have been told repeatedly that the extraterrestrials want to help us evolve while preserving the free will of humans to make decisions for themselves. I began by asking a guide if there really was an agreement among the advanced cultures of the galaxy and our planet. His reply was quite positive.

There is an agreement for peace and cooperation for all beings.

My next question was, "Do the governments here on Earth participate with this agreement?"

As far as you have governments, yes.

I get the impression that the guides do not have a lot of respect for our governments. When I inquired if aliens look at other governments with more favor than they look at the United States, he replied:

No, you are all seen as one.

Notice that he was not making his opinion of what they thought of the world governments known. At the present time, violence around the world is growing at an alarming rate. I asked if the advanced cultures would get involved if a major war was to break out among human governments. His reply was a bit disheartening.

They allow you to create your own destiny.

I guess if they let more than 60 million people or three percent of the world population die in World War II, they will pretty much stand by and let human nature take its course.

History of the Treaty

I assumed that the treaty has been around for quite a while. When I asked if one of our presidents made the first treaty, he answered:

I do not know my history well but early 1800s. After Washington. Close, he died early. Like number 10.

William Henry Harrison was the ninth president of the United States. It was very cold and he gave a 105-minute inaugural address without wearing a hat. He caught pneumonia giving the speech and died thirty days later. Hard to believe he had time to communicate with aliens, but I guess anything is possible. His vice president, John Tyler, took over in 1841, and finished the term. Maybe he was the first to negotiate an understanding with our alien neighbors. In any event, it seems as though the agreement in the form of a verbal understanding has been around for a long time. When I asked when the first formal treaty was negotiated with the United States, the reply was:

1943.

That was in the heart of World War II and Nazi Germany was preparing to use their rocket technology learned from the Bavarian crash of 1938. Our military must have been very concerned. I asked who negotiated the treaty on the part of the United States.

Eisenhower.

It would certainly be appropriate for the Supreme Allied Commander to participate in such a discussion. When Harry Truman took over as president, he was actually recorded as saying the following (www.collective-evolution.com):

Oh yes we discuss it at every conference that we had with the military, and they never were able to make me a concrete report on it. . . There's always things like that going on, flying saucers and they've had other things, you know.

You can actually go onto YouTube and hear the above quote in his own words. Eisenhower was assuredly involved in the negotiations with the aliens of the time.

The Terms of the Treaty

If indeed such an agreement exists, there must be only a few people in very high places who know the terms. One evening we were channeling with Mou, and I brought up the subject of a treaty with the galactic committee. When I asked him what was in the treaty, he said:

We will let you alone if you let us watch.

My guess is that his statement pretty well sums up the whole secrecy situation. People ask me all the time if aliens are evil. I try to explain to them that they are so advanced, if they meant us harm, we would be harmed. Very few people have any idea that a treaty exists with the alien community.

Hopefully, the terms of the treaty will act as a control over other countries. When I asked if the terms of the treaty were so strong that the governments of the world would kill innocent people to protect it, he replied:

Yes.

That answer did not do a lot for my personal peace of mind. I hope the information I am passing on is not in violation of a treaty of which I have no knowledge. My next question attempted to clarify some of the details. "Why do you guys insist on secrecy about beings from other planets being present around us?"

It is agreed by many, but times are changing.

The interesting part of that answer is that "times are changing." In an attempt to better understand the terms of the treaty, I asked him to explain the basics.

You agreed not to tell about us. To let us walk among you. Do studies on you and to do our own manipulation. There is a lot more I cannot tell you.

It would be interesting to know what aspects of the treaty he would not disclose. My guess is his comment was part of him dumbing down the information for my safety. I was curious why they were so determined to keep their presence a secret. His answer made a lot of sense.

Fears. Today people run on fear. Look what occurred when on the radio, a play came on about aliens attacking. Just a play and people killed themselves. It was kind of a test to see what you might do. Well, we all know only the crazy believe in ghosts and aliens.

He was referring to the George Orwell *War of the Worlds* broadcast that took place in 1938, that created panic throughout the country. I guess it was clear at that time that alien disclosure would not be well received by the general public. Hopefully, we are more prepared for the information now.

Free Will, For Better or For Worse

When I asked if they would let us use nuclear weapons against each other, the reply was:

No interference.

I sincerely hope humans are around to travel the stars sometime in the future. Next, I inquired if hostilities broke out between extraterrestrials that were members of the treaty, how the governing council would react.

They would stop it.

Those answers are pretty clear clarification that the human race is on its own when it comes to survival decisions. The committee would intervene to stop a war between advanced cultures but not on Earth.

A Minor Intrusion

I asked how long they have been watching us.

You have to remember we have been here when three manlike animals roamed the planet. We watched your last Ice Age. We have let your planet evolve with only two or three major intrusions.

So they have been observing our planet before souls were present in the current human form. I could not help but wonder just what would be considered a major intrusion to an alien, so I posed the question, "What is an example of a major intrusion?"

I am not versed in this as much as I should be, but I know we sent advisors to teach young scientists about atom splitting. You figured out hydrogen.

You made a bomb and you were warned not to. You set it off and just about destroyed Earth. We had to stop it.

I am old enough to remember testing the hydrogen bombs. My next question addressed how the extraterrestrials stopped us from destroying our planet when we exploded a hydrogen bomb.

Deprived it of fuel by introducing an opposite fuel. Your scientists are just learning this. For everything there is an opposite. Like sound has an opposite. If you broadcast an opposite sound you get no sound. It is silent.

In case anyone was doubting just how advanced the beings from other planets really are, we were just told they are capable of reversing the effects of a hydrogen bomb. Apparently, the treaty also provides that the aliens will help us in other ways. I posed the question to Mou, "Are there any other benefits for us?"

We volunteered knowing about genes. And we helped understand stealth.

I have no doubts that there is a lot more he cannot tell us.

Enforcing the Agreement

While I am on the safety thought, I asked him one night if the terms of the treaty were so strong that it encouraged our government to assassinate innocent individuals to prevent disclosure. He replied:

We cannot condone killing.

I assume there is a difference between condoning and participating. The aliens do not condone killing, but that does not include the governments—they do. Unfortunately, there are many instances where witnesses have decided to commit suicide shortly after being interrogated by government officials. Probably the best example of individuals committing "suicide" occurred following the Rendlesham Forest incident in Great Britian where members of the military observed an extraterrestrial craft and beings over a period of several nights. When British intelligence interviewed the individuals who had observed the incident, the men were told "bullets are cheap." I asked Mou if the British Men in Black ever killed anyone to prevent them from talking about the incident. His reply confirmed my beliefs.

Ha, ha, ha, ha.

Not exactly the answer I was looking for. When I asked him what he thought was so funny, he ducked my question by answering:

It was against your agreements. Have other ways they were told to use.

I asked Mou if the galactic committee would ever let our governments tell the truth about the presence of extraterrestrial beings; he refused to answer the question. After I restated the question and inquired when the truth about the alien presence would become known, he replied:

Not now. There are many variables.

With the coming of the age of the Internet and rapid communication, it seems that the alien presence is becoming more and more difficult to keep a secret. During a session, I asked Mou how many years it would be until disclosure took place. This time he gave me a definitive answer.

3 years.

Using this writing as base, that would equate to the year 2020. If he is indeed correct, it should be a very exciting year.

A Whistleblower Tells of the Treaty

Apparently, Eisenhower had continuing negotiations with the extraterrestrials that resulted in a formal agreement in 1954. There are multiple versions of the meetings leading up to the agreement by Eisenhower and the terms negotiated in it. William Cooper was on the briefing team for the Commander of the Pacific Fleet from 1970 to 1973, and had access to the classified documents concerning the treaty. Here are his own words. Note the similarity to the terms that were told to us by Mou.

> The treaty stated that the aliens would not interfere in our affairs and we would not interfere in theirs. We would keep their presence on Earth a secret. They would furnish us with advanced technology and would help us in our technological development. They would not make any treaty with any other Earth nation. They could abduct humans on a limited and periodic basis for the purpose of medical examination and monitoring of our development, with the stipulation that the humans would not be harmed, would be returned to their point of abduction, would have no memory of the event, and that the alien nation would furnish Majesty Twelve with a list of all human contacts and abductees on a regularly scheduled basis.

There are various interpretations of the treaty available online, but they all contain the same basic terms. It is nice to have independent verification. I find it interesting that our government has elected to allow the alien visitors to conduct testing on citizens of our country without their approval. I guess when you are trying to negotiate with advanced cultures that could wipe out our entire planet in the wink of an eye, you are at a severe disadvantage to get what you want in a negotiation.

Abductions, Study Allowed by Treaty

In the preceding paragraphs, you have read that a whistleblower pointed out that abductions are allowed by our treaty with the committee. When I asked Mou if they were covered in our agreement, he replied:

Yes.

"Do you have to get permission to conduct abductions?"

No.

"Are they considered the main method for extraterrestrials to study humans?"

Yes.

However, when I attempted to get more information about the process of studying humans without their permission, he interjected another thought.

Abducting your terms. We prefer to call it teaching.

He was obviously referring to the positive aspects of the process. I asked if there were any other terms that applied to the process.

Cooperation.

Connie and I are aware that we have both been involved with interactions with aliens in the past. When I asked when our sessions had taken place, he replied:

While sleeping and we prefer to call it teaching.

"Have there been other teaching events?"

Multiple. You are all being taught, not abducted to use your term. Do not be frightened as your word abduction suggests.

"Should we think of it as attending a class where we are given information?"

Many are being taught.

When I inquired how long a class lasts, he answered:

A lifetime.

Maybe humans are just slow learners. I figured I would get a little more personal information. "How many classes have we had?"

Throughout your lives.

We have known from previous sessions that Connie had been physically taken in the past. When I asked if I had been physically taken, he replied:

No, do not take.

One obvious fact is that Connie and I have been spending a lot more time with extraterrestrials than we ever imagined. There is a lot more going on out there concerning the governing structure and pecking order of our galaxy. We are all under the control of a governing committee and a treaty that most of us have no idea exists. Hopefully, some day it will all become public knowledge; it would be really nice to be aware of just how manipulated our lives really are.

Then I asked, "Have extraterrestrials ever impregnated a female during an abduction?"

No.

"Does it take a special vehicle to conduct a human abduction?"

No.

"How long does an abduction last?"

Varies.

"Do the abductors usually speak to the victims during a normal abduction?"

No.

"Do they communicate mentally?"

Sometimes.

I now inquired if more than one type of extraterrestrial conduct learning sessions.

Many kinds.

"What type of aliens conduct the most abductions?"

You work with.

Mou is a blue alien from the planet Robbe and he is the spirit that we have been working with for the past couple of years. In an earlier session he had admitted that he was present in the vehicle when an abduction had taken place, but he said the he had not personally participated. I asked if he was saying that Blues conduct the most learning sessions. His answer ducked the question.

We don't measure. It is a blending of conciseness.

We were also told that if a person has a physical problem at the time of an abduction, the extraterrestrials will heal the illness. I believe that this is what happens when individuals find out that they have been suddenly cured of a major illness. In any event, Mou considers the taking of a human, either physically or mentally, a positive occurrence.

CHAPTER 9

HISTORY OF ALIEN ACTIVITIES ON EARTH

In my previous book *Aliens Among Us: Exploring Past and Present*, I went into great detail explaining how the extraterrestrial beings have been among us and influencing the evolution of mankind from the time of the dinosaurs. In that book, I pointed out references to aliens in the Bible, discussed the Nazca Lines in Peru, and many other examples of alien influences in the past. Every day more and more evidence is coming forward making their past presence irrefutable. I thought I would include some of the more interesting proof that was not in the previous book. Hopefully, this past evidence will strengthen some of the information about the beginning and evolution of mankind.

Ancient Alien Activity

Mou has told us that aliens observed our last Ice Age, the time of the dinosaurs, and the evolution of man. That covers a very wide time period. Dinosaurs roamed the Earth from 230 to 65 million years ago, and the first human remains date to about 195,000 years ago. Our last Ice Age period began around 2.6 million years ago, give or take a few years. One thing is for sure, visitors from other planets have been observing what was taking place on Earth for a very long time. Humans as we know them are relatively newcomers.

One theory is that the age of the dinosaurs ended when a large meteorite struck the Earth and the residue of the strike blocked out the sun. This lack of sunlight resulted in lower temperatures and the killing of the vegetation. The combination of events proved lethal to the largest beings to ever roam our planet. Maybe the extraterrestrials decided that it was time to give someone else a chance to develop and directed a meteor toward the Earth. When I asked Mou if aliens were behind the meteor crashing into the Earth that killed the dinosaurs, he replied:

No, natural causes.

So much for that theory!

Water and Our Earth

Life on Earth would not be possible without the presence of water, especially since the human body consists of around sixty percent H_2O. One of the great mysteries concerning our planet is how our Earth came to have so much water. It seems logical that a planet would just be a mass of solid rock, not have the majority of the surface covered with water. I asked if water was present on our planet at the time of creation. He replied:

It was but in different form.

"What form was it in at creation?"

Gas.

"How did the gas that was present become water?"

Falling temperatures.

At the time of formation, our planet must have been very hot. Keep in mind that the core temperature of Earth is still similar to that of the sun. I followed up by asking, "So you are telling me that as the Earth cooled, the gas condensed into the water that formed our oceans?"

Yes.

The formation of our oceans appears to have taken place through a natural process, not with any alien assistance. We had been told before that a liquid presence is one of the requirements for intelligent life throughout the universe.

Keep Trying

Next, I inquired how many years ago extraterrestrials first visited Earth. His answer to that was:

90 million years ago.

That time frame is during the era of the dinosaurs, precisely what he told us before! There is a huge gap in time from when extraterrestrials first visited Earth to when humans finally arrived. We should consider the possibility that there could have been early cultures whose remains have totally disappeared. I asked if there was ever a time that there was a civilization on our planet that consisted only of extraterrestrials. He replied:

Yes.

"What was the name of the type of alien that was on Earth that long ago?"

Patanps.

"Are we familiar with that type of alien?"

No.

I hope they waited until after the dinosaurs were extinct to start their colony. Having a T-Rex for a pet would be an adventure. I was aware from past sessions that there had been numerous attempts to "seed" an intelligent race on our planet. I asked how many attempts had been made here on Earth.

5.

It was becoming obvious that our visitors from other planets certainly had perseverance. My next question was, "How many years ago was the first attempt made to seed intelligent creatures on Earth?

350,000 years.

That would make the first seeding attempt around 150,000 years before the first traces of man. We had been told earlier that the first attempts at creating intelligent life on Earth took place in the sea. I asked why the attempt was made in the sea rather on land. He replied:

Ingredients.

My guess is the composition of the ocean and our atmosphere was probably different in those days. When I asked Mou if there were any earlier form of humans before the establishment of Homo Sapiens, he answered:

Yes, not Homo Sapiens.

"If they were not Homo Sapiens, where did they live?"

In the sea.

"Are you saying that early attempts at creating intelligent forms were in the sea, like fish?"

Some.

There are definitely different life forms in the sea that are mammals, so I asked him if dolphins were descendants of that attempt at creating intelligent life?

Yes.

I had not thought about it before, but there are actually several types of sea mammals including whales, manatees, seals, sea lions, and walruses. My guess is they are remnants of the early attempt at seeding intelligent life on Earth.

Seeding Humans

On numerous occasions, our alien guides have referred to attempts to create intelligent beings on Earth as "seeding." At what point do they decide to throw in the towel and start over again? My guess is there are a lot of seeds out there in the universe. In any event, aliens have been steering the development of the human race for a very long time, apparently since its inception.

In a later session, I decided to reexamine the concept of how there were multiple seedings of humans through time as extraterrestrials attempted to create a race on Earth with advanced intelligence. On this evening we had another guide that was familiar with our distant history. I mentioned that we were told in the past there was a culture on Earth that consisted only of aliens. I was totally unprepared for his answer.

These beings are your humans.

When I asked if he was saying that we all evolved from an alien culture, he reinforced his earlier answer.

You call them aliens, we do not.

The guide had a point. If all souls are the same, the only difference is the shape and location of their bodies when in incarnate form. I attempted to follow up on his statement by asking, "What do you call them?"

What you call human beings.

Our guide was giving us information that would have Charles Darwin turning over in his grave. His last statement does not exactly correspond to the concept that man slowly evolved from apes. I reiterated to him that our studies of evolution indicate that the present human form started out a couple of hundred thousand years ago as an early form of ape, and then I asked if that was truly how man evolved. He replied:

No, it has been a process.

"Are you saying that evolution did not take place as we are led to believe?"

This time it did.

If I am understanding the guide correctly, an alien form was brought to Earth and then evolved into the human form we are today. "Do you consider humans in their current form as advanced beings?"

In the works.

That was a polite way of saying that we have a little more work to do, but we do seem to be advancing. It seemed to me that it would have made sense to have created man as an advanced form from the beginning rather than go through all this 200,000 years of evolution. When I asked the guide why they just did not go ahead and seed a more advanced form, he answered:

Oh, but we have. This is not your first go.

He did say earlier that there have been five attempts to create the human race. To better understand what he was saying, I asked if all aliens had DNA.

Yes.

"Do all humans have alien DNA?"

Yes.

We were just told that all humans have beings from other planets as distant ancestors. When I asked if the evolution of the human form to its present form was the result of extraterrestrial inbreeding, he replied:

Less physical.

In an earlier chapter, we learned that it is impossible to tell certain alien types from humans. Apparently sexual interactions were not the entire key to human evolution.

Keeping the Human Ship Afloat

My guess is that if humans had attempted to evolve during the time of the dinosaurs, they would have wound up as appetizers. I asked him if aliens have ever arranged natural disasters to help determine what forms of life evolved on our planet. He responded:

Of course, but only as long as in physical form.

In order for the human race to prosper and expand, I would think that there had to be a little protection provided by our friends from outer space. I asked him if aliens ever had to intervene to save humans from extinction. His answer was:

Two events required reseeding. Survival was possible but we aided.

"What were the two events?"

Asteroids.

Asteroids have been a major problem for life on this planet; the dinosaurs could testify to that.

Sumerians and the Anunnaki

Sumerian figure. Adobe Stock.

What is considered the first civilized society, the Sumerians, only came into existence around 6,500 years in the past. The Sumerian or Mesopotamian culture thrived between the Tigris and Euphrates rivers in southern Iraq and is considered the first great world culture. They invented the world's first writing system, invented the wheel, an active religious system, mathematics, and agriculture methods very advanced for the time. It is reasonable to ask how, after millenniums of hunting and gathering, a civilization is formed that had large cities and a strong governmental system in a relatively short period of time. I believe that the visitors from other planets got tired of waiting for humans to develop on their own and decided to give us an information boost. I have included several carvings from the Sumerian era that have some rather strange details. For instance, the images displayed here show an individual holding some type of a water bucket and seems to have a pair of wings. Keep in mind that only a few generations earlier, they were painting on the walls of caves. This type of detail in their artwork is a huge advancement.

Sumerian figure. Adobe Stock.

A common image associated with the Sumerians is that of a bearded male with wings, usually holding a type of pocket book or maybe a water bucket. When I asked Mou if that was an image of the Anunnaki, he replied:

No.

Surprisingly, when I asked him if they were living beings, he answered:

Yes.

"Is that type of being still alive?"

Doubtful.

"What was the name of the life form with the wings and beard?"

Yodrum.

That was not a name with which I had any familiarity. In another image, a figure with an eagle-type head has the same type of wing design and is also holding the same type of water bucket. Since this is a book on aliens, it would be only natural to think that advanced beings from other planets might have lent a hand to the Sumerians in showing the tools for cultural advancement. When I asked if the people of Mesopotamia were helped in the advancement by beings from other planets, Mou answered:

Yes.

"Were the Anunnaki visitors from other planets?"

Yes.

"Were they from the mystery planet Niberu?"

No.

"Were the Anunnaki the extraterrestrials that taught the Sumerians their technological advances?"

Yes.

The Sumerians were the first great culture to record events and images by means of wall carvings. I always assumed these often bizarre carvings represented the aliens that came to assist their culture. I was surprised with the reply when I asked Mou what the Anunnaki looked like.

You.

If they looked like me, they must have had double chins and bald heads! "You are saying that the Anunnaki, the aliens that assisted the Sumerians, looked just like humans?

Yes.

The Sumerians are generally credited with inventing the wheel, a major breakthrough for the time. I asked Mou if the Anunnaki helped with the invention of the wheel. He answered:

Yes.

Mesopotamians were also among the first to have a written language. When I inquired if the aliens were instrumental in teaching writing he replied:

In part.

There is a lot of conjecture about the origins of the Anunnaki. "Where did they come from?"

Frolp.

"I assume that is from a planet that humans have never heard from."

Yes.

Another theory is that the Anunnaki still walk the Earth. He also put an end to that idea when the answer was:

No.

Extraterrestrials contributed to the rapid advancement of the culture in ancient Mesopotamia. We confirmed that the Anunnaki were the alien culture that provided that assistance.

Atlantis

The existence of the lost civilization of Atlantis has been discussed for many years with its location being anywhere from Bermuda to under the Antarctic ice. Plato mentioned an island nation in his dialogues "Timaeus" and "Critials" that he called Atlantis. He referred to it as a very advanced culture that sank into the ocean around 9,600 BC. In Plato's writings, Atlantis was described as a huge island located beyond the Strait of Gibraltar. He mentioned that he had heard the story from his grandfather who had heard it from an Egyptian priest. Since the first Egyptian dynasty only dated to around 4,000 BC it is doubtful that the Atlantis referred to by Plato ever existed. When I asked Mou if Plato was correct, he replied:

No.

When I inquired if the ancient civilization named Atlantis really existed, the answer was:

Yes.

"When was the time of Atlantis?"

3000 BC.

This would have been around the time of the Egyptian dynasties and the Sumerian empire. This was also the time of a lot of extraterrestrial activity on Earth. I asked if extraterrestrials played a large role in supplying information for the development of Atlantis. The answer was:

Yes.

"Where was Atlantis located?"

In the Atlantic sea, near Bermuda.

"Is the current island of Bermuda part of the land mass that was Atlantis?"

No.

"What happened to Atlantis?"

They were using crystal power, and they had an atom bomb-like mishap. They were in ways more advanced than you.

"Is the land mass that was Atlantis currently under water?"

Yes.

"What made their land sink under the Atlantic Ocean?"

Earthquake.

"Is there any evidence of their culture remaining today?"

Buildings.

"Are they under the water?"

Yes.

If the buildings of this ancient culture still exist today, it is possible that some day in the future the remains of their culture will be discovered. I was curious how many people lost their lives when Atlantis ceased to exist. When I asked the peak population, the answer was:

1 million.

That is a lot of individuals for an early culture. My next question was, "Did anyone survive?"

No.

According to Mou, Atlantis was a very advanced culture for their time. They were destroyed by a catastrophic explosion as a result of their use of a crystal power technology that was supplied to them by alien visitors. As a final question, I asked Mou if our souls had ever reincarnated on the island of Atlantis before their demise. He replied:

No.

It would have been interesting to have recalled a prior life in that ancient city.

First Recorded UFO Sighting in America

The first recorded sighting of what appears to be a UFO in the United States dates to 1639. The Puritan governor of Boston, John Winthrop, recorded the event in his official journal. The sighting was shared by multiple people, but the description included below is attributed to James Everell, a person described as being sober and a person of good reputation. It took place over the Charles River in Boston. For this to be a recorded event, it would have had to be of major proportions. Not only was there a sighting, but their light boat was moved over one mile against the tide. Here is the official entry (www.celebrateboston.com):

> In this year one James Everell, a sober, discreet man, and two others, saw a *great light* in the night at Muddy River. When it stood still, it *flamed up*, and was about three yards square; when it ran, it was contracted into the figure of a *swine:* it ran as swift as an arrow towards Charlton [Charlestown], and so up and down [for] about two or three hours. They were come down in their lighter about a mile, and, when it was over, they found themselves *carried quite back against the tide* to the place they came from. Divers (many) other credible persons saw the same light, after, about the same place.

I have no clue what happened when it took the shape of a swine or pig. It would be quite interesting to know what went through the minds of the individuals involved in the sighting. Keep in mind that the vernacular of the time was not capable of describing such an event. When I asked Mou what the objects were that were sighted in the Boston Harbor, he replied:

> *Orbs.*

I was hoping he would say space vehicles. I then asked if the sightings were alien related, and he answered:

> *No.*

In this instance, I think paranormal activity has been mistaken for an extraterrestrial happening.

Nazca Lines of Peru

Nazca Lines of Peru. *Adobe Stock.*

Nazca Lines of Peru, the monkey. *Adobe Stock.*

In my previous book, I discussed Peru's Nazca Lines in detail. In my mind, they are the best examples of absolute proof of the existence of ancient aliens on Earth. Located in southern Peru, these geoglyphs or images etched in the sand extend over 386 square miles (1,000 square kilometers). Some of the figures are huge and defy any explanation other than assistance from extraterrestrial beings. The multiple figures consist of more than 10,000 lines. In order to fully appreciate the images, you have to see them from the air, which brings up the question of how they could have been created by ancient people without access to aircraft.

In past sessions, we spent a lot of time talking about the various formations or shapes, and Mou had been quite helpful in telling us what they stood for. One image that I could not define was the monkey. Not only was the image huge, it did not seem to make any sense. When I asked Mou the purpose of the monkey shape, he said:

Was simple landing strip, even though you think otherwise.

He was even reading my mind! I guess the message is never to mess with an alien spirit. I am sorry I did not think to ask him what kind of vehicle would have landed on such irregular runways. You can view these formations from your computer by bringing them up on Google Earth. You will find them well worth viewing.

The more I communicated with Mou and other guides, the more I realize that we all owe our current existence to the intervention of extraterrestrial beings. Hopefully they will continue to help us evolve in the future and not just write humans off as either too stupid or violent to ever travel the stars.

CHAPTER 10

EXTRATERRESTRIAL ACTIVITY PRESENT AND FUTURE

In this chapter I will discuss some of their current activities and then try to get out my crystal ball and see what lies ahead for humans and our alien partners. While free will seems to be the largest deterrent to the advancement of our culture, hopefully our alien visitors will continue to lend their assistance. One evening I asked Mou what beings on other planets currently wanted for the human race. He replied:

Survival and evolution.

"Why do extraterrestrials want the human race to advance?"

You choose.

"How do we choose?"

To rebuild.

"What do we choose to rebuild?"

Your species.

I think he is trying to tell us that we may also choose not to advance by means of our misuse of free will. As we learned in previous chapters, earlier forms of humans failed to evolve here on Earth. In my mind, one of the largest deterrents to the advancement of the human race is our proclivity for violence and wars. While wars can be a very effective method of population control, it could also cause the extinction of humans by means of a nuclear apocalypse. When I asked if aliens would ever intervene to end war, the answer was:

No.

Apparently the futility of war is a lesson we will have to learn for ourselves. My belief is that if other intelligent planets in our galaxy can learn to live together, we might be able to learn as well. I inquired how many years it would take for humans to learn to live peacefully together, and his answer was not very comforting.

That remains unknown.

That certainly seems to rule out peace in my lifetime. At an earlier time, he gave us another statement that seems to indicate there is a long learning road ahead.

There is always going to be conflict and in conflict we learn compromise. This is now what your world is evolving into. Through war we learn peace.

Peace may indeed be the most difficult subject that humans have to learn in the future. It will be very difficult to evolve in human form if we are all dead.

What Do Aliens Want of Humans?

Since Mou was a Blue alien in life, I figured he would have a good idea of just what the rest of the galactic community wanted of our human race. When I asked the question in another way, his reply was:

We are here to help you. We do not want your planet. We have our own thank you, and we do not want to harm you. This is all nonsense that we want what you have. We are here to make sure you can make the leap when you are ready.

I was not sure why mankind was going to need to make a leap. When I asked what he was referring to, he replied:

In the space time continuum there are as many virgin planets waiting to be settled or create their own karma as there are dead and worn-out planets ready to be re-eaten by its suns. The planets are on a timer. They are born, they thrive, and then they die. It is the way of things. In a few more billion years this solar system will be all burned up. Not from mans' misuse but just because that is the way of things. If we are to survive we learn to travel the stars. This is how and why you must learn not to depend on Earth forever. We are here to make sure you grow towards this.

That kind of sucks for our planet in the long run but at least we have a little time before the shit hits the fan. It seems like humans are advancing technologically at a very rapid rate. Our government is currently talking about an expedition to Mars. I was curious just how long it would be until earthlings could travel freely among the planets. He answered:

150ish.

No question I will not be around to see it.

War and Peace

We have heard repeatedly that our neighbors from the rest of the Universe want the human race to evolve and advance. One evening I asked if they favor any country over the United States at any time in the future. His reply was quite optimistic.

No, they desire peace for all mankind alike.

"If you want peace for all of humanity, would you get involved if a major war broke out that threatened to destroy large segments of our population?"

They allow you to create your own destiny.

"Will there be a major war in the future that will radically reduce our human population?"

That is not our call.

It was becoming obvious that interplanetary visitors take very seriously the right of humans to exercise their free will, even to the point of making decisions that would lead to their extinction.

Current Activities

An overriding theme of this book is the incredible extraterrestrial activity that takes place, unseen, around us every day. It seems logical that as a part of this activity, there would be places used on a regular basis as a landing site for smaller alien vehicles. One evening I asked if the guide would tell me some of the most used locations. He replied:

Desert.

"What country are you referring to?"

New Mexico.

That was not exactly a country but the State of New Mexico definitely has a lot of desert. I know it is not in New Mexico but it is in the desert, so I asked if Area 51 is one of their landing sites.

At times.

I knew this was a stupid question but I asked if our government is aware of the use of Area 51 as an alien landing site. He answered:

Yes.

"Does our government cooperate with them?"

Yes.

"Has this cooperation with our government been going on for a very long time?"

Not so long, 50 years.

While fifty years may not be a long time for a spirit guide, this is quite a while our government has been misleading us. It looks like the conspiracy theorists have been correct for quite a while about Area 51. I asked if there was another base where we were working together with other beings. He replied:

Under the sea.

I had read somewhere that there was a base in the Pacific off Catalina Island. I asked if that was the location and his answer was:

No. In the trench.

That would certainly be a hard-to-find location. It is safe to assume that there are numerous areas where our governments are cooperating with beings not of our planet. These locations would be among some of the most closely guarded secrets. My next question inquired if there are any other places where extraterrestrials and humans were working together. He replied:

Yes.

"Where are the largest facilities where they are working together?"

West.

We had already discussed Area 51. I suggested Dulce Mountain, another rumored site.

One, also LA Bay.

Dulce Mountain is in New Mexico, near the Colorado border. We had been told before about a base off Catalina Island. The more we inquire, the more information we receive concerning either alien bases or cooperation with humans. Apparently, there is a lot more cooperation than any of us imagined.

Future Colonies

As I am writing this book there is talk about NASA considering a program to colonize Mars. I know that with Earth's early state of space exploration, such a project would be a major feat. When I asked Mou what would be the first planet to be colonized by humans, he replied:

I think you will see Jupiter and Pluto, which is still a planet.

He seemed a little upset that we did not consider Pluto a planet any more. His answer caught me off guard, so I asked him if he was saying that we would colonize them before Mars.

I say that you will be visitors.

That makes a lot more sense than trying to colonize them.

Cooperative Effort

If history is any indication of future actions, our advancement in space travel technology will be heavily dependent upon cooperating with extraterrestrials. When I inquired what species was currently taking the lead in working with humans, the answer was:

Tiny whites you would call them.

"What do they do?"

Work on behalf of humans.

"What is the main location where aliens and humans are working together?"

No location.

"What type of projects do they work on together?"

Not working on projects.

"If they are not working on projects together, how do they interact?"

Not together.

I could see that this line of questioning was not going anywhere. I changed the subject by inquiring what countries were currently taking the lead in cooperating with extraterrestrials.

US and Switzerland.

I was not expecting Switzerland, but they do have a long history of neutrality and diplomacy. My next question was, "Is there ever a time that the advanced cultures will lose patience and take over our government?"

No.

At least they are going to let humans dig their own grave, so to speak.

Alien Disclosure

We know that the presence of extraterrestrials is a secret that is required by the treaty and enforced by the committee. We also know that we have been told that circumstances are changing. With all the communication advancements, there will have to be a time in the future where the alien presence will become public knowledge.

It will be very interesting to see how the general public reacts to that realization. But what happens after disclosure? I inquired what changes would take place after public disclosure. His answer was:

Beings will work together.

I heard a rumor that there were areas off our planet where extraterrestrial beings were already working with humans. When I asked if that was true, the reply was:

Yes.

"What is the location?"

Akruln.

"Is that on Earth?"

No.

Apparently there really is some truth to cooperation outside of our world. I had asked in an earlier session how long it would be until humans could travel the stars recently but I was interested in verifying the information from another guide. He answered:

200 years.

Mou had told us earlier that it would be 150ish years until we could travel the stars so it looks like it will take another eight generations or so to learn the technology. I inquired as to the most important technology to learn if humans were to make the huge leap, and the answer was:

Time travel.

Humans have an awful lot to learn before we take our place in the advanced culture community.

A Personal Encounter

One evening in 2015, the presence of a real extraterrestrial became up close and personal. At the time, Connie and I were renting an apartment near our store in Pennsylvania. It was late at night, and she and I were asleep. Something woke me up and I sat up in bed. We always sleep with a night light, and as I looked to my left, I became aware of a form standing by the side of the bed, looking at Connie as she was sleeping.

Thinking I was possibly dreaming, I shook my head to make sure I was really awake. What I was seeing in the dimly lit room was not your average image. It was large, standing nearly seven feet, and had a reptilian appearance. Its arms were short and it had a short mouth, almost resembling that of an alligator. As I watched, he turned his head toward me and seemed to smile. That is the last image I remember, and I must have lost consciousness. When we awoke in the morning, I told Connie that I thought I saw an alien and it was standing by her side of the bed. She asked me how much I had to drink before I went to bed. I did not have the heart to tell her the alien smiled at me.

A couple of nights later, we channeled by Skype with K and Doc in Salt Lake City. They were on the board and I was asking questions. I made no mention of what had taken place in our bedroom. We started the session by asking if it would be possible to have Mou present. After we confirmed his spirit was really with us, I asked if I had really seen a real alien in our bedroom. He answered:

Yes.

At least I wasn't dreaming. I inquired if I was taken during this visit. He replied:

No travel, just a look.

I guess that was good news. My next question was, "Did he knock me out after I got a good look?"

After you got a nice look, yes.

"Was he a Gray?"

Yes.

"He looked like he was around seven feet tall."

Yes.

I then told Mou that he looked right at me, and I saw his eyes. He then reiterated what I had seen but mentioned to no one.

He smiled.

He just told me that a real gray alien smiled at me! Absolutely no one, including Connie, knew that had happened. My next question was, "That all happened before he put me back to sleep?"

Yes.

"I thought it was very cool."

Yes.

"Was it good that I did not show any fear?"

Yes.

I guess if you are going to write books about the alien presence, it is a good thing to personally be able to vouch for the fact that you have actually seen one. Mou verified everything that had happened on a channeling board more than 2,000 miles away, being operated by individuals that had no knowledge of the events that had taken place. That is pretty good confirmation!

Alien Contributions

Through the years, visitors from other planets have contributed many technological advances to the evolution of the human race. I think it is safe to say that we would not be watching television and listening to smart phones without the alien contributions, probably beginning with the original seeding of humans. During a session one night, I asked what was the greatest contribution that aliens ever performed for the human race. I was not prepared for his answer.

Provided oxygen.

"Are you saying there was a time when Earth did not have oxygen in its atmosphere?"

Yes.

"How did they provide the oxygen?"

Beyond your understanding.

I do not think that any of their contributions will be any greater than providing oxygen. In multiple sessions we have been given many technical innovations contributed by extraterrestrials through the ages; here are some of them:

The wheel and writing for the Sumerians
Technology for construction of the Pyramids for the Egyptians
Rocket technology for Nazi Germany
Atomic energy for the United States
Medical advancements working through humans such as the Salk Polio vaccine
Provide concepts such as wormholes for Einstein
Discovery of radio waves
Information concerning genes and DNA
Stealth technology
MRI machine
Miniature cameras
Rocket technology for the United States
Optical cable
Atomic power
Radiation
Wind Mills
Sonic energy

The list really just scratches the surface of the number of advances that have been given to us by alien visitors. When I attempted to discuss some of the medical advances given to us, he replied:

We keep trying.

While that answer certainly opened the door for more discussion, I asked if the pharmaceutical industry was the culprit in keeping us from getting additional cures. His answer was:

No, human will.

We have been told before that the human greed for money has caused many medical advances to be withheld. It is more profitable to treat an illness than to cure it.

The contributions of beings from other planets are uncountable. It is possible that mankind might not even be present on this planet if it were not for the presence of the advanced cultures throughout the galaxies. Cooperation in the future will be instrumental in humans being able to travel the stars and advance to actively join the other intelligent cultures.

CHAPTER 11

MISCELLANEOUS MYSTERIES OF THE UNIVERSE

As I come to these final chapters, there is a huge realization that we have only begun to scratch the surface and to understand the knowledge concerning our universe and the beings that reside in it. We know so little of the miracles taking place around us that the sum of our intelligence could be compared to a baby taking its first steps. In this chapter, I will attempt to address some of the miscellaneous subjects that might be of interest to individuals and have not been covered elsewhere. One of the first items to be investigated will be the infamous Planet X or Nibiru.

Nibiru

This is a subject that gets intense debate on the Internet. Believers argue vehemently about the existence of the mystery planet while our government argues that it is a figment of their imagination. Of course NASA argues vehemently that Nibiru absolutely does not exist, and if it did we would have been tracking it for the last ten years. Everybody knows we can trust NASA and take anything they say to the bank! I asked Mou if the planet of Nibiru really existed and his answer was:

Yes.

I must admit I was among the doubters on this subject and quite surprised by his answer. For those of you who have never heard of Nibiru, an author named Zecharia Sitchin wrote a book originally released in 1976, named *The 12th Planet*. It is believed that the twelfth planet mentioned in his book is Nibiru. It is said to have an elliptical orbit of 3,600 years that will bring it close to Earth, causing serious or maybe even apocalyptic consequences. Sitchin believed it was home to the Anunnaki, and when it came close by, they moved to Earth. I asked if there was ever any ancient life on Nibiru.

No.

So much for it ever being the home of the Anunnaki. Next, I asked, "Will it ever get close to Earth?"

Yes.

"Is Nibiru the ninth planet?"

Yes.

"How does the planet compare to the size of Earth?"

Earth is smaller.

I was hoping this thing was going to be a lot smaller than Earth. Many theorists say that the passing of such a large celestial object will cause earthquakes here on Earth. My next question was directed to the effect the passing would have on our planet.

Areas may change.

"How will areas change?"

Border of oceans rise.

"Will the passing of the planet cause earthquakes?"

No.

"Why does it not show up on our telescopes?"

It does.

"How many years will it be until the presence of Nibiru will be confirmed?"

45 years.

If the passing of the planet is inevitable, you have to wonder why the government is keeping its presence a secret. I got a clue why the passing of Nibiru is so low on the NASA priority list when I asked how long it would be until Nibiru passed by Earth. He answered:

36,000 years.

That certainly put it pretty low on my worry list.

Planets and Beings Like Earth

When humans speak about life on other planets, they tend to think that extraterrestrials will be in their own likeness. Up to this time, all of the acknowledged alien types were not anything like humans unless you refer to the shape changers. I asked Mou if there were any beings in our galaxy that were similar to humans. He returned my question with a question.

In body?

"Yes, in body."

Yes.

"Where are they located?"

Cvap.

I guess he took it for granted that I would know where Cvap is located. I asked him if it was a planet in our galaxy.

Yes.

I inquired if they were more advanced than we were.

Yes.

I think everyone is more advanced than we are. I asked, "Can they travel the stars?"

Yes.

"Are they more peaceful than we are?"

Yes.

So there is definitely a chance that someday a craft will land and individuals will get out that look just like us. I changed the subject and asked if there were any other planets in our galaxy that were similar to Earth with an atmosphere and water. He answered:

Yes.

"How many?"

9,000.

As he said before, just think of the possibilities.

Hollow Earth or Flat Earth

If you go on the Internet, you will find multiple websites that claim Earth is hollow, and there is an intelligent culture living there that will someday emerge to lead earthlings into the future. When I asked Mou if the Earth was hollow, his reply was:

No.

So much for the hollow Earth folks! While I was at it, I asked if the Earth was flat. The guide thought I had lost my mind and replied:

Silly question.

My assumption is that means no. Even though we discussed our moon earlier, I thought I would ask a few more detailed questions.

Activity in Our Solar System

It appears that there is quite a bit of extraterrestrial activity going on in our own solar system. Our moon, located only 238,900 miles from Earth would be a great place to have a supply base for operations on Earth. When I asked Mou if aliens had a current operating base on the moon, his reply was:

No, we moved out when you came but the astro belt and Mars, Jupiter, and I think Saturn. Some planets are solid. Some are thin as an egg shell and some are in between. The thicker the surface, the more likely life. Solid planets are not good either. You have no pushing and pulling so you have mountains and such.

In 1969, Buzz Aldrin and Neil Armstrong made our first moon landing and got a good look for themselves at what was already there waiting for them. Although this transmission was blocked from the public by NASA at the time of the moon landing, a former employee of the space agency, Otto Binder, states that ham radios around the world picked up this transmission.

NASA: What's there?

Mission Control calling Apollo 11 . . .

Apollo 11: These "Babies" are huge, Sir! Enormous! OH MY GOD! You wouldn't believe it! I'm telling you there are other spacecraft out there, lined up on the far side of the crater edge! They're on the moon watching us!

While I am on the subject of our moon landing, there are many that say our presence there was staged for the world to see. When I asked Mou if our first moon landing was fake, he said:

No, we saw it; it was real.

At least NASA was truthful about us going to the moon, just not what our astronauts witnessed while there.

This Santa Claus Does Not Have a Sleigh

Another very interesting incident took place as part of the Apollo 8 mission when James Lovell orbited the backside of the moon. As Lovell emerged from the backside of the moon on Christmas morning, he sent the message back to NASA, "Please be informed there is a Santa Claus." Skeptics might say that this message was meant to be part of a Christmas message, but it is also rumored that Santa Claus was the code name for aliens. The use of the name of the jolly fat man in a red suit would certainly not arouse any curiosity from the general public. Once again, the dirty little secret of alien presence would be kept a secret. When I asked Mou if Lovell had seen aliens on the back side of the moon, he answered:

Yes.

We had been told before that aliens observed our moon landing.

Play That Funky Space Music

The Apollo 10 mission that blasted off from Cape Kennedy on May 18, 1969, was the last mission before attempting the moon landing. Astronauts on this mission were Thomas P. Stafford, John W. Young, and Eugene A. Cernan. While orbiting the backside of the moon, they claimed they heard an "outer space-type" music that was coming from the space module's radio. Here is the transcript that came from recently declassified NASA transcripts.

"The music even sounds outer-spacey, doesn't it?" one of the astronauts said. "You hear that? That whistling sound? Wooooo?"

"Sounds like . . . you know, outer-space type music," another of the men said.

The strange sounds continued for almost an hour before they stopped. After the mission ended, the transcript was declared to be classified and remained a secret for many decades. This is but another example of our government assuring that they were living up to their side of the treaty.

Tabby's Star

Located a mere 1,480 light years from Earth in the Cygnus constellation is a star with the official designation Star KIC 8462852 that has become known as Tabby's Star. What makes this star so interesting is that the light shining from this celestial body has diminished by twenty percent from 2011 to 2013, and tends to flicker erratically. This has never been recorded for any other star. It is almost like some huge body is blocking the light from being seen here on Earth. One theory is that there could be a huge alien-made structure that is orbiting Tabby's star. Of course it is also possible there could be space dust or debris blocking the view. In any event, what is causing the diminished light is one of the great current space mysteries. I asked Mou if he was familiar with Tabby's star and he replied:

Yes.

The idea of a mega-structure blocking the light from the planet has a lot of attraction for the space conspiracy people. When I inquired if there was a huge structure associated with Tabby's star the reply was:

No.

"What causes Tabby's star to dim?"

Rotation.

"Can you clarify what you mean by that?"

Revolutions are slow.

We all know that our planets rotate around the sun, but did you know that our sun itself rotates? Not only does it rotate, but since it is not a solid object, it rotates faster at its equator than it does at the star's poles. According to the guide, Tabby's star does not rotate like other stars and is relatively stationary.

A Deep Space Fleet

At the time of my writing this book there is a conspiracy theory going around the Internet that the United States has a fully operational fleet of space vehicles, and that we have totally explored our solar system. There have even been claims that our country has had a colony on Mars for the past twenty years. A great-granddaughter of President Eisenhower even claims she was recruited to become a resident of the colony. In another article, I read that the project was given the name "Solar Warden." When I asked Mou if the United States had a secret deep space fleet the answer was:

No.

I followed up by asking if our country was involved in an operation called Solar Warden. Once again he said:

No.

I think we can safely dispel the rumor of a deep space fleet and an active colony on Mars. This news is going to be quite a disappointment for many. Even though "Solar Warden" is a myth, we have been told there is cooperation outside our planet.

Black Holes

Artist concept of a black hole. *Dollar Photo Club.*

We have all heard the term "Black Hole," but I am sure very few of us really know what a black hole in space represents. All stars in the Universe have a life span. In time, every star in space, including our sun will burn out from exhausting its fuel and die. According to existing theory, when a star runs out of fuel it collapses upon the core. The act of collapsing concentrates matter and creates the black hole. When the dying sun collapses, it creates a pull of gravity so strong that not even light can escape. Since you cannot see an absence of light, the area appears black. Anything near the collapsing star will be sucked into that black hole by the intense gravitational pull.

A black hole. Adobe Stock.

According to NASA, the term "black hole" is a misnomer. It is actually not a hole but an area where gravity has tightly packed a huge amount of matter within a very small area. The example used on their website is to think of a star ten times more massive than the Sun squeezed into an area approximately the diameter of New York City. That concentration of mass is what creates the incredible force of gravity, so strong that not even light can escape it. The mechanics of how that all takes place is far beyond my comprehension. Scientists estimate that there are as many as ten million to a billion such black holes in the Milky Way alone.

One night I asked Mou, "What is a black hole?" and he replied:

It is an energy vortex that sucks you in one side and spits you out the other side of time.

I guess that is one way of describing what happens. My next question was; "What happens if a spaceship gets sucked into a black hole?"

They get smashed down and spit out on the other side, but smaller, condensed.

"Is everyone killed?"

So far no one can figure that out.

Some of the stars in the Universe are immense, much larger than our sun. As a means of comparison, our sun is 1,000 times larger than our largest planet, Jupiter, which in turn is eleven times larger than Earth. When one of those large bodies implodes, the black hole that is created can destroy an entire galaxy.

The result is a gravitational field so strong that nothing, not even light, can escape. In recent years, NASA instruments have painted a new picture of these strange objects that are, to many, the most fascinating objects in space. I read somewhere that black holes were really portals to other dimensions. When I asked Mou if that was true, he answered:

No.

So much for that theory.

Understanding Black Holes

I think it is safe to say that no one fully understands the inner-workings of a black hole. One evening I decided to attempt to understand the un-understandable with a different spirit guide. I started by asking the guide just exactly what a black hole was.

Energy density.

That answer seemed to make a lot of sense. I read somewhere that a black hole is formed when a star "burns out." I started by inquiring if that was true.

No.

When I asked the guide how a black hole forms, he answered:

Dense energy.

"What causes the dense energy to become a black hole?"

Rotation, rapid movement.

I also read that the gravitational pull is so great that light cannot escape the void that is created. His answer to that was:

No, light passes through.

"Does it make the light accelerate?"

Yes.

It seems to me that a black hole would have two ends. All the books talk about matter being sucked into the void so it appears logical that matter would be sucked in from both ends to the middle where only God would know what happened to it. When I inquired whether energy was sucked into the black hole from both ends, he answered:

It exists within.

"What happens to the energy in the middle?"

Energy is formed and accumulated within and expands out.

"What form does the energy take when it is expelled from the black hole?"

It has no solid form. It expands as to become more of the same.

At this point I had no clue what he was talking about. He might as well have not said anything and that it was just beyond my understanding. As a parting question on this subject, I inquired if what I learned in physics class, that energy can be neither created nor destroyed, was correct.

Yes.

I will leave this to far better minds than mine to sort out. I changed the subject and asked if there were any black holes near our own solar system. His answer kind of ducked the question.

Near is relative.

When you are talking in terms of light years, he is correct. My follow-up question was, "Do any black holes threaten our galaxy?"

No.

Thank goodness for that! During my lifetime, there have been multiple meltdowns in nuclear facilities. In my research, I ran across an article saying that in essence, the meltdown of a nuclear facility was the same process as creating a black hole. I asked the guide if that was true.

Similar.

I found that answer very chilling, especially after Three Mile Island, Chernobyl, and the Fukushima Daiichi nuclear disaster. His answer was equally as chilling when I inquired if Earth could be destroyed as the result of a meltdown of a nuclear reactor.

Life forms only.

I guess it is comforting to know that the planet will still be here, just devoid of life.

Dark Matter and Dark Energy

If you really want something that will mess with your mind, try to do some research on dark matter or dark energy. In previous sessions, Mou told us that our concept of space was incorrect.

Space that looks empty to you is really filled with a fluid like substance, yet solid.

At the time he made that statement I had no idea what he was talking about. I thought space was this huge vacuum of nothingness. While doing the research for this book, I started to attempt to understand dark matter and dark energy. NASA states that dark energy makes up nearly sixty-eight percent of the universe but that they really cannot define what it is. Dark matter makes up around twenty-seven percent but they also cannot define it. The remaining five percent is made up of what we call ordinary matter, i.e., planets, asteroids, suns. That means that ninety-five percent of our universe is unexplainable.

It is generally agreed upon that our universe is expanding, perhaps even at an increasing rate. However, since gravity exerts a force that tends to pull things together, you would think that the huge pull of suns and planets would make the universe get smaller. Therefore, the idea is that there is some kind of energy that counteracts the gravity and pushes the suns and planets apart. Our scientists have not as yet been able to prove that such a type of energy exists.

One explanation given by NASA for dark energy is an undefined dynamic energy fluid or field. I guess I should have taken Mou seriously when he said space was filled with a fluid-like substance. When we asked for more information concerning dark energy, I came to the realization that this was going to be a very difficult subject to understand. I started by inquiring, "What is dark energy?"

More dense.

"What is more dense?"

Energy.

"What type of energy is more dense?"

You could not comprehend.

That answer is always a good way to end a conversation. I tried to gain a little more information by asking if dark energy only occurs in interstellar space. I guess he figured I could understand this answer.

It does not on Earth.

It gets really interesting when you attempt to sort out dark matter. If it has solid particles there would be an absorption of radiation that could be measured. If it was a type of anti-matter there would be some type of emission as it collided with matter. If it was a huge black hole, there would be indications of objects being attracted to it. Whatever the matter is, it had no color, so therefore, the term "dark matter." The reality is the composition of dark matter is one of the great space mysteries.

On another evening with a different guide, I started by asking, "What is dark matter?"

Dead gasses.

"So you are saying that the dark matter in the universe is simply dead gasses."

Just a density. Just older density to universe. Matter is density.

There is a theory among astronomers that dark matter keeps the universe from collapsing upon itself from its own gravitational attraction. He did not agree with the theory when I asked if it was correct.

No.

"What is the purpose of black matter?"

Deflection.

"Can you explain what you mean by 'deflection?'"

Gathers particles that might otherwise be harmful.

My guess is that answer is not overly helpful in describing black matter. I give the guide a lot of credit for at least attempting to give me information I might understand.

Life in Other Dimensions

Humans are very comfortable living in their three-dimensional world without ever considering that there may be unseen dimensions with a lot of activity going on around them. If you spend any time on the Internet you will be introduced to the concept that there may even be a parallel universe. One evening, I asked Mou if there was a parallel universe, and he put the end to that rumor by answering:

No.

If you read my book *Spirits Speak of Conspiracies and Mysteries*, you learned that Bigfoot actually lives and occupies a multiple-dimension world. That is the reason their bodies have never been located. I pointed out to Mou that he had discussed life in other dimensions so I asked him if he would explain them for us. It was a subject he did not want to discuss and he replied:

No.

Looking for a reason for his negative answer, I suggested that the reason for his answer was because it was beyond our understanding. He said:

Yes.

I thought that if I rephrased the question, he would discuss the subject. He once again answered:

No.

I should have known from previous experiences that asking the question in a different manner rarely helps. If you have read any books such as *We, The Arcturians*, you will find out that they refer to themselves as fourth- and fifth-dimension beings. I asked the guide if he could explain the fourth dimension.

It is not a place but rather a way.

"What are you referring to as 'a way'?"

Of being open to more of all there is.

This line of questioning was going to become difficult to understand. I asked him how a human opens one's self to enter the fourth dimension. His answer was a bit of a parable.

All of that which you do not know. You are all so busy being human. Humans do not allow.

"What is it that humans do not allow?"

Practice that which allows expansion, love.

I was beginning to understand what he was referring to in the characteristics of humans. I inquired if he was saying that eliminating negative energy would allow us to enter the fourth dimension. He replied:

Yes, being present not always in your Earthliness.

He was once again pointing out that earthlings have a bit of room for improvement.

A Real and Current Danger to Earth

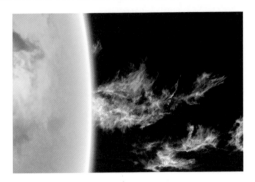

A CME, or coronal mass ejection, from our sun. *Adobe Stock.*

How many of you are familiar with coronal mass ejections or CMEs? If you really want something to worry about, this is it. They are actually giant clouds of solar matter that are ejected from the sun and are capable of creating havoc with our GPS, satellites, and especially our electrical power grid. The sun is constantly undergoing storms that result in solar flares, sometimes accompanied by strong solar matter ejections. A strong ejection striking Earth is not a matter of *if*, just a matter of when.

In 1859, our planet was hit by a strong CME that became known as the Carrington Event. It was so strong that the telegraph lines actually caught fire, disrupting what at that time was the most advanced form of communication. If we were struck by such an event today, it would wipe out our satellites, of which there are more than 1,100, and overload our power grids creating a devastating blackout of power and communication.

It is estimated that such an occurrence, though rare, is a "one in one-hundred-year event" and the probability of it happening in any one year is between two percent and twelve percent depending on the sunspot activity. Since it has been more than 150 years since an event took place that has a probability of occurring every one hundred years, it is safe to say we are overdue. In 2012, there was an ejection similar in strength to the Carrington Event that narrowly missed Earth. If it had happened one week earlier, Earth would have been directly in the crosshairs.

I asked our spirit guide if there was going to be a CME similar to the Carrington Event in the near future and he answered:

No.

That was good news for Earth. Next, I inquired if he could tell us how many years in the future such a similar event would take place. Once again I consider his answer good news.

I am not seeing such.

In the event of a nuclear attack, there would be an Electromagnetic Pulse (EMP) that would be similar to a Coronal Mass Ejection, (CME). An EMP caused by an atomic blast would affect individual pieces of equipment such as cell phones and the computer equipment controlling our electrical grid. I asked our guide if there was going to be an EMP attack in the near future and he replied:

No.

Even though our guides predict there will be no CMP or EMP attacks in the near future, situations can change, and I did not get him to define what he meant by "near future." We should all be prepared for unforeseen emergencies or natural disasters at any time.

Nebula

Butterfly Nebulae. Adobe Stock.　　Rosette Nebulae. Adobe Stock.

As our abilities to peer into deep space increase, astronomers have been able to photograph some of the most amazing and beautiful features in space, the Nebula. Named after the Roman name for "cloud," they are the places where stars and planets are born. We are told the clouds consist of dust, plasma, helium, and hydrogen gases. Space is not really a vacuum but widely dispersed particles and gas. These particles can start to attract each other and undergo a type of gravitational collapse. As these materials clump together, their gravitational pull increases, and the process of attraction is accelerated. These nebulae are immense in size and can actually measure hundreds of light years in width. Our universe goes through processes of death and rebirth, much like the reincarnation of humans, only on a much grander scale. I asked our guide what really is a Nebulae.

Your simplest terms, it is a life form.

Eagle Nebulae. Adobe Stock.

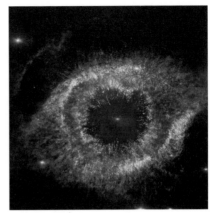

Helix Nebulae. Adobe Stock.

He was obviously in the process of dumbing down my information. When I inquired as to the type of life form, he reiterated his respect for my ability to understand.

You would not know this.

In an attempt to rebuild my ego, I tried a different approach. "Our scientists say it is a sun forming. Is that correct?

Not entirely.

I don't think he holds our scientists in very high regard either. When I asked him to clarify his last statement, the reply was:

It contains ingredients for creating life as you know it.

In this instance, I thought I would quit asking questions while I was ahead. As the technologies of the human race increase, many of the answers to these mysteries will become known and considered commonplace. For the current time, there should be amazing discoveries in the future that will lead to us being able to travel the stars and observe these mysteries up close and personal.

CHAPTER 12

ANTARCTICA

The Continent of Mystery and Aliens

The continent of Antarctica has always been a mystery to me until I started to write books concerning extraterrestrials. In my earlier book, I wrote about the existence of Nazi bases and the encounters of Admiral Byrd with extraterrestrials on the ice continent. Admiral Byrd's encounter was named Operation Highjump and took place in 1947, when his armada of ships and 4,000 men encountered alien craft. The isolated continent has a long history of extraterrestrial interactions. We were even told that the Admiral's death may have been related to keeping the information of what happened to his task force a secret.

Did you know there is actually a treaty concerning Antarctica that was ratified by the United States in 1959? After WW2 and with the beginning of the cold war with the Soviet Union, there was fear that the continent would be militarized and even be used for nuclear testing or weapons storage. By the 1950s, seven nations claimed territorial sovereignty and eight others had done scientific exploration but had not made claims. Article 1 of the agreement states:

Antarctica shall be used for peaceful purposes only. There shall be prohibited, inter alia, any measures of a military nature, such as the establishment of military bases and fortifications, the carrying out of military maneuvers, as well as the testing of any type of weapons.

This agreement is still in effect today, but there is a lot going on that may be infringing on the terms. As a passing thought, I did not notice anywhere that the aliens were a part of this treaty.

Geologic History

Around 200 million years ago an ancient super continent existed that included the land masses of Africa, Antarctica, Australia, India, and New Zealand. At this time, dinosaurs ruled the world, and the continent was covered in lush vegetation. Forces began to separate the land masses and the South Atlantic began to form. By 95 million years ago Antarctica had broken free, enjoyed a semi-tropical climate, and continued to drift south. Around 65 million years ago a meteor struck Mexico, and the dinosaurs become a thing of the past. By that time, Antarctica had a cooler climate, like that of the current UK.

Around 25 million years ago the continent became covered in ice. Fossilized plants have been found from as recently as 2 million years ago that indicate the ice sheets have advanced and melted many times over the ages. Apparently global warming is not an entirely new phenomenon. Since we have been told that extraterrestrials have visited this planet since the time of the dinosaurs, it would not be out of line to think that they might have visited and maybe even colonized this continent in the past.

A Mapping Mystery

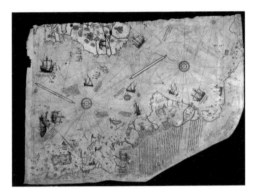

Piri Reis Map, Circa 1513.

Oronteus Fineaus Map, Circa 1532.

As I finished this book, the icy continent began to be in the news more and more, and I started to do some additional research. The first interesting objects I discovered were sixteenth-century maps of Antarctica that showed the land mass that is currently under thousands of feet of ice. From my short geologic dissertation, I think it should be obvious that Antarctica was covered with thick ice in the sixteenth century and many years prior.

The earliest map was drawn by a famous Turkish admiral named Piri Reis in 1513. It was drawn in great detail on animal skin. In a series of notes on the map, he admits accessing the Imperial Library of Constantinople that contained cartography information dating back to the third or fourth century BC. This early information is contained on his map. Keep in mind that the earliest time this area was free of ice was around 4,000 BC, and the first documented discovery of the ice continent took place in 1771, by Captain James Cook. That is quite a discrepancy in time.

There is a second map called the Oronteus Finaeus map that was drawn in 1532, that shows the continent of Antarctica completely ice-free and in amazing detail. An obvious question is how could a map of this detail be constructed without access to satellite information or modern mapping methods? Perhaps there may have been a little help from our visitors from another planet. However, when I asked the guide if the information was provided by extraterrestrials, the answer was:

No.

When I pressed them to find out who provided the data for the maps, the guide ducked the question and refused to give me a direct answer. As we have learned before, there are just some answers that will not be provided by the other side. In any event, there have been no accurate answers to how these maps could have been drawn 250 years before the continent was discovered and 5,500 years since parts of the continent were ice-free.

Antarctica: The Alien Crap Hits the Fan

As I write this chapter in the spring of 2017, we are becoming aware of discoveries in Antarctica that have the potential to change how we think about beings from other planets. The Internet is full of conspiracies ranging from the discovery of huge pyramids and archaeologists exploring the remains of an ancient alien culture, to a huge stone stairway, reminiscent of the construction of the Mayan pyramids. It is even reported that our Secretary of State John Kerry and agents of the Vatican, had rushed to the frozen continent in late 2016. Whatever is taking place, it seems like the events might be hard to keep from the public. When I asked the guide what was happening in Antarctica, he replied:

Got a problem with aliens.

Now that is an answer that aroused my curiosity. I inquired what kind of a problem and he said:

Your pres, TV.

My guess is that the powers that be think our President Trump will make an announcement on television about the alien presence. We have been told by the spirit guides that disclosure will take place by 2020, and maybe our new President may be the one to spill the alien beans.

I was aware that there were alien colonies on the continent of Antarctica in the past, so I asked if one had been recently discovered. He ducked the question.

Vow of secrecy.

It sounds like this event is definitely covered by the terms of the treaty. In light of what the guide just informed me, it is quite understandable that the presence of our secretary of state would be required. I asked why John Kerry went to Antarctica.

I think it is safe to assume it was not to make snow angels near the South Pole. The guide answered:

A duty.

"Why the secretary of state?"

A different direction forward detected.

That would appear to be an understatement. It sounds like our secretary of state had to do a little rapid negotiating. I inquired if President Trump had been briefed on the presence of an alien colony. He replied:

Yes.

"Will he disclose the presence?"

No.

"Was he briefed that disclosing the information would be in violation of the treaty with the committee?"

Yes.

As we discussed earlier, the treaty has very far-reaching terms and penalties. Next, I asked, "Will the information of the presence be leaked in the future?"

Yes.

I guess if the information is not intentionally disclosed but leaked, the committee will not be as upset. From his answers, I think it is safe to assume that our government will do their best to continue to keep the presence a secret. I decided to try to find more information about what had taken place, so Connie and I got back on the channeling board to clarify some of the previous replies. I started by asking if the guide could provide me with more information about our problem with the aliens in Antarctica. He replied:

A dust up.

Next, I inquired if we uncovered an alien base. His answer was:

Yes.

There have been theories on the Internet that the incident was a little more serious than a "dust up." When I asked if a fight broke out he said:

Yes.

"Was anyone killed?"

Yes.

I could tell from the brevity of his answers that getting information was like pulling teeth. My next question inquired, "Was our military involved?"

Yes.

"How many members of our military were killed in the incident?"

140.

"How many did you say died?" I wanted to make sure we had gotten the correct message.

140.

That was the exact number we had been given in the previous answer. I asked how many aliens were killed.

None.

I have said all along that if the extraterrestrials meant us harm, we would be harmed. Apparently our military weapons are no match for theirs. I inquired if the killing of the humans was accidental.

No.

I was of the impression that the treaty prevented this type of deadly interaction between humans and extraterrestrials. My next question was, "Did the aliens have the permission of the Committee to kill humans?"

No.

"Are the aliens that were involved going to be in trouble for breaking the rules?"

Yes.

From the information we have been given, the beginning of hostilities would certainly be a change in policy direction. I asked if these would be the events that would force disclosure.

Yes.

We had been told several times earlier that disclosure would take place within three years (of the writing of this book).

It will be very difficult for our government to keep what has taken place a secret for very long. My next question was if what was happening was good or bad for humans.

Good.

While violence is harmful in the short run, disclosure will open the way for cooperation between humans and extraterrestrials in the future and unleash huge jumps in technological information.

Pyramids in the Antarctic

Antarctic Pyramid. *Google Earth.*

Recent discoveries seem to indicate the presence of pyramids very similar to those found in Egypt and other countries. Thanks to Google Earth, we are able to check them out for ourselves. I was curious if they had any relationship to all the current activities in Antarctica. I asked if what is happening with the aliens was related to the pyramids that have recently been discovered.

No.

There was a time many millions of years ago when the continent of Antarctica was located in a warm climate. Movement of the tectonic plates through time moved the land mass to the South Pole. I asked if the pyramids were built when the land mass was in a warmer climate. The answer was:

No.

"How many years ago was were the pyramids constructed?"

20,000.

That means the construction took place in an extremely cold environment and was long before what was believed the first advanced civilization in Mesopotamia, the Sumerians. I inquired if they were built by aliens.

Not entirely.

"Did aliens help?"

Yes.

"What was the purpose of these pyramids?"

For bearings.

We had been told before that the pyramids around the world had crystals on their tops that were used to help alien ships of the time to navigate around Earth. I asked if these pyramids had crystals on top of them when they were built.

Yes.

"Are the pyramids related to what is currently occurring with the alien dust up?"

No.

Apparently the pyramids have lost their usefulness as alien technologies advanced through time.

Antarctic Alien Entrances

Antarctic alien entrance. *Google Earth.*

We have been told in various sessions that there are underground alien colonies in Antarctica and there are cave-like entrances that allow access to them. The advent of Google Earth allows amateur conspiracy theorists to examine the most rural parts of our Earth for signs of alien activities. One evening I asked our guide if there were entrances to underground extraterrestrial bases in Antarctica. He replied:

Yes.

I included an image of what certainly appears to be some kind of an unusual underground entrance. Through the miracle of Google Earth you can view the entrance for yourself. It almost looks like the entrance was designed for a saucer-shaped ship. When I asked the guide if my photograph was that of the entrance to an alien base, he replied:

Yes.

Even the most ardent skeptic should admit that the photograph shown here is a bit unusual to be found in the wilds of the Antarctic. I asked if the alien colony existed at the South Pole. He replied:

No.

"Is the base that was discovered near the South Pole?"

No.

The coordinates of the entrance are not near the South Pole, even though there have been articles written about a no-fly area that is supposedly an alien base located in the vicinity of the pole. When I asked if there really was an extraterrestrial base in Antarctica, he replied:

Yes.

So the base is just not near all the human activity located near the South Pole.

Antarctic Alien Aircraft

We have been told on numerous occasions that there are alien aircraft on the continent of Antarctica. On one occasion, I inquired if there were indeed alien ships that are permanently hidden there. He replied:

No.

Not exactly the answer I was expecting. Connie interjected that maybe they were just located in plain sight. When I rephrased the question the answer was:

Yes.

"Are humans aware of the extraterrestrial vehicles?"

Yes.

I have included a photograph from Google Earth that appears to show the outline of a saucer-shaped vehicle sticking out from an overhang or cave. Apparently the beings from another world have little or no fear of being discovered.

An Archeological Dig

Photograph of alien vessel. *Google Earth.*

There are a lot of rumors that archeologists have been digging for some very strange remains in Antarctica for several years. The rumors are that an ancient culture of aliens were flash-frozen and buried under thousands of feet of ice. When I asked if the dig was looking for ancient aliens, he answered:

No.

When I asked if the dig was for an ancient human culture he replied:

Yes.

This is a really strange place for a human culture to exist, especially since it has been covered by ice for 6,000 years. I asked if John Kerry had visited the dig.

Yes.

I thought I would throw a curve ball, so I asked if Kerry saw alien remains. The guide answered:

No.

He was definitely consistent that the remains were not from another planet. Another indication from the Internet was that the individuals were very tall. When I asked the average height of the individuals found in the dig, he said.

9 foot.

I could see why the scientists would think the remains were aliens. I asked if President Trump was briefed that the remains were not alien.

Yes.

That would be a good reason for the president not to disclose that an alien colony was discovered under the ice. It is quite possible that one of the most remote and inhospitable places on Earth will play a huge role in all of our futures and may even be instrumental in forcing the world to realize that there is a current and real alien presence. Disclosure in three years may be a real possibility.

CHAPTER 13

CONCLUSION

I find it is very hard to write a conclusion to a book that seeks to tap a source of information that to humans is never ending. Because of the agreement between world governments and the committee, we know so little about the alien presence around us that we are like babies emerging from the womb. The general belief is that the people would panic if told the truth of the aliens around us.

Earthlings are such a young culture in relation to other beings in the Universe, and our level of understanding is so low we are often even incapable of asking intelligent questions. When we are given answers, in many instances we are either incapable of understanding or accepting them. In spite of the growing evidence of the existence of life on other planets, around fifty percent of the people still refuse to believe we are not alone.

An obvious first step to understanding the alien presence is to accept the concept that extraterrestrials truly exist and in fact are visitors to our small planet. I would hope that in this book we have at least managed to get the reader over the hurdle of believing in an extraterrestrial existence. The next and very difficult step is attempting to understand the activity going on around us. Admittedly, it is very difficult to understand something denied by our government and cannot be seen or presently understood.

As I have attempted to explain, the most important concept to understand is that our visitors are here to help humans evolve to the point that we can join the more advanced cultures, and they mean us no harm. There will be a time when our planet, because of natural occurrences, will become uninhabitable and travel among the stars will be required to preserve the human race. Past attempts at seeding the Earth with intelligent beings, capable of evolving and surviving, have failed. Hopefully this human form can learn the lessons of the past, learn love and respect for others, and continue positive evolution. It is also important to realize that because of free will there are no guarantees.

While respecting our free will, the goal of the alien beings is to lead us in the direction of cooperation and understanding. That is a lesson learned by the advanced civilizations long in the past. Until we learn these lessons, humans will be delegated lower-level members of the galactic community.

We have been told repeatedly that there are emotions that humans have never felt and, therefore, can never understand. There are dimensions that exist that we have never seen as well as languages that human ears have never heard. It is impossible for us to contemplate space travel where molecules are transported by methods we never imagined over distances we cannot even define. Humans are attempting to catch up with cultures that have a head-start on earthlings by not only thousands but millions of years.

An overriding theme of this book has been that various extraterrestrial types are cooperating in attempting to help humans advance in their evolution. I am sure you were as surprised as I was when Mou stated there were more than 250 alien types involved with a single space vehicle dedicated to exploring our solar system. As I stated earlier, the extraterrestrials are so advanced that if they meant us harm, we would not be able to intervene. If they wanted our stuff, they would have our stuff. The reality is that our weapons, quite capable of creating Armageddon on our planet, would be ineffective against their technology. If they can travel at speeds in excess of twice the speed of light, while avoiding space debris or meteorites at those speeds and orbit our planet without being observed, they could easily destroy life on Earth if they so desired.

The reader should also take comfort in the fact that the galaxy is governed by a committee that protects underdeveloped planets like Earth. In addition, our world governments are well aware of their presence and have agreed to a treaty that gives our planet additional protections. Unfortunately, that treaty also assures that they can observe us without disclosure of their presence. They are also allowed to conduct testing to better understand how humans are attempting to kill themselves. Someday that will change but only when we can understand and accept the truth.

We also examined the spirituality of our galaxy and found that advanced beings share beliefs in the same deity as we do here on Earth. On Mou's planet, more than a hundred light years from Earth, they even celebrate a holiday similar to our Christmas when God sent his son to other planets as well. It is comforting that the advanced cultures have learned to play nice together and get along, proving that there is even hope for our planet.

No one can understand or visualize the immensity of the universe. As our technology increases and we gain the ability to observe more distant galaxies, we find out how little we really know about our universe. The human race is on the road to traveling the stars, and I think we can anticipate some bumps in that pathway. My goal has been to introduce you to the possibilities that exist in the physical and spiritual world around us. Mou has informed us that civilized cultures have only explored five percent of the known universe. There are literally millions and perhaps billions of planets with intelligent life. As we have been told, think of the possibilities.

BIBLIOGRAPHY

https://exopolitics.org/archived/Study-Paper-8.htm.

https://science.nasa.gov/astrophysics/focus-areas/what-is-dark-energy.

https://solarsystem.nasa.gov/planets/earth.

https://solarsystem.nasa.gov/planets/jupiter.

https://solarsystem.nasa.gov/planets/jupiter/moons.

https://solarsystem.nasa.gov/planets/mars.

https://solarsystem.nasa.gov/planets/neptune.

https://solarsystem.nasa.gov/planets/pluto.

https://solarsystem.nasa.gov/planets/saturn.

https://solarsystem.nasa.gov/planets/uranus.

https://solarsystem.nasa.gov/planets/venus.

https://space.stackexchange.com/questions/13051/what-prompted-lovell-on-apollo-8-to-announce-there-is-a-santa-claus.

https://truedisclosure.org/news/solar-warden-inception-to-present-day.html.

Milanovich, Dr. Norma J. *We, The Arcturians.* Albuquerque, New Mexico: Athena Publishing, 1993.

Roseberry, Dinah. *Psychic Pets: Solving Paranormal Mysteries.* Atglen, Pennsylvania: Schiffer Publishing, 2010.

Strohm, Barry R. *Aliens Among Us: Exploring Past and Present.* Atglen, Pennsylvania: Schiffer Publishing, 2015.

www.americaspace.com/?p=28284.

www.ancient.eu/atlantis/.

www.ancientdestructions.com/oronteus-finaeus-map-antarctica-fineus/.

www.astronomy.com/news/2017/06/jupiters-new-moons.

www.astronomy.com/news/2017/10/whats-going-on-with-tabbys-star.

www.bbc.com.

www.bibliotecapleyades.net/universo/esp_sirio13.htm.

www.bibliotecapleyades.net/vida_alien/alien_races01a.htm.

www.buddhanet.net/e-learning/5minbud.htm.

www.celebrateboston.com/ufo/first-ufo-sighting.htm.

www.collective-evolution.com/2016/05/04/ president-eisenhowers-great-granddaughter-speaksabout-his-meeting-with-extraterrestrials/.

www.collective-evolution.com/2017/05/13/theyre-parked-on-the-side-of-the-crater-theyre-watching-us-when-neil-armstrong-landed-on-the-moon/.

www.dailymail.co.uk/sciencetech/article-5093449/Conspiracy-theorists-claim-Nibiru-destroy-Earth.html.

www.earlychristianwritings.com/gnostics.html.

www.himalayanacademy.com/readlearn/basics/nine-beliefs.

www.history.com/news/history-lists/9-things-you-may-not-know-about-the-ancient-sumerians.

www.livescience.com/2410-council-nicea-changed-world.html.

www.nasa.gov/audience/forstudents/k-4/stories/nasa-knows/what-is-a-black-hole-k4.html.

www.newshub.co.nz/home/world/2017/11/nazis-and-pyramids-what-s-really-going-on-in-antarctica.html.

www.nydailynews.com/news/national/apollo-10-crew-heard-outer-space-type-music-article-1.2539046.

www.ourhollowearth.com/.

www.popsci.com/does-moon-sound-like-bell.

www.rt.com/news/310459-nasa-ufo-sun-aliens/.

www.sciencechannel.com/tv-shows/through-the-wormhole/.

www.sitchin.com/.

www.skepticreport.com/sr/?p=156.

www.space.com/20881-wormholes.html.

www.theancientaliens.com/433000-years-of-annunaki-rule.

www.ufocasebook.com/Hill.html.

www.universetoday.com/54756/what-is-the-big-bang-theory/.

www.universetoday.com/61103/what-is-a-nebula/.

www.urbandictionary.com/define.php?term=beam%20me%20up%20scotty.

www.worldatlas.com/articles/the-glaciation-timeline.html.